"*Grieving for the Sibling You Lost* is a groundbreaking book, giving a much-needed voice to the experience of sibling death—one of the most unacknowledged and minimized losses today. This book does a wonderful job of providing tips, tools, and coping strategies on how to find hope and meaning after a sibling loss. It is a must-read for bereaved siblings who want to gain a better understanding of the sibling experience. I wish I had this book when my 17-year-old brother died."

—**Heidi Horsley, PsyD, LMSW, MS**, executive director of Open to Hope Foundation, and adjunct professor at Columbia University

"All too often there can be a painful, silent scream inside the heart and mind of a teenager who has lost a sibling. The terrain of adolescent development is difficult enough as it is, yet when a brother or sister of a teenager dies, life changes forever and becomes emotionally complex and tumultuous. In this book, Erica Goldblatt Hyatt presents a deeply compassionate and empathic understanding of the teenager's grief experience. The guidelines offered herein offer a knowledgeable road map of the journey of healing and recovery. Goldblatt Hyatt is a skilled traveller providing signposts and directions along the uncharted terrain of healing from the loss of a sibling. This book is a very readable, user-friendly, and practical resource for any teenagers walking the mourner's path, and for those who accompany them."

—**Simcha Paull Raphael, PhD**, founding director of the DA'AT Institute for Death Awareness, Advocacy and Training

"A clear, helpful, experience-near book, this is useful not only for teens grieving the loss of a sibling but also for parents of adolescents. ... Written in a simple way, teens can identify with the way grief feels, think about their own feelings and behaviors that are normalized, and gain some understanding of the undertow of grief. A well-written and very direct look into the life of adolescents who face profound losses."

—**Joan Berzoff, MSW, EdD**, professor and director of the
  End-of-Life Certificate Program, Smith College School
  for Social Work

"Erica Goldblatt Hyatt provides a wonderful resource that can help teens understand what grief is, the symptoms that often accompany it, and the various ways to cope with sibling loss. Using real stories of teens who have suffered sibling loss, this book gives teens support in a very real and relatable way. Teens of all ages will be able to use these stories as guides to help them understand and make meaning of their own grief experiences."

—**Mary Alice Varga**, assistant professor of educational
  research at the University of West Georgia, and
  active member of the Association for Death
  Education and Counseling

"Grieving for the Sibling You Lost is a first-rate guidebook for navigating one of life's most painful experiences, the death of a brother or sister. The book speaks to teenagers as they try to come to terms with the confusing emotions associated with loss. This pioneering work by Goldblatt Hyatt offers practical guidelines and enlightening advice for teenagers, their parents, teachers, and clinicians. I recommend it highly."

—**Raymond Moody, MD, PhD**, best-selling author of twelve
    books, including *Life After Life*, and coauthor of *Life After Loss*

"Grieving for the Sibling You Lost by Erica Goldblatt Hyatt is a most excellent book. The book is amazingly written in a style that is both intimate, informative, and inspirational. What I found especially wonderful is the range of readership is so inclusive. This classic book is readable for young people who have lost their brother or sister, as well as for a professional person like myself who has been a psychologist and psychotherapist for many years. Reading this most interesting book brings you into this experiential matrix that is affectively informing, and in which the reader simultaneously experiences a personal connection with the author. I recommend this book not only for its informative content but also for the pleasure of reading an exquisitely written text."

—**Rudolph Bauer, PhD**, diplomate in clinical psychology at the
    American Board of Professional Psychology, The Washington
    Center for Consciousness Studies

"*You are not alone*. This is the promise that Erica Goldblatt Hyatt so skillfully makes and delivers to you in the pages of this remarkable book. She takes you on the journeys of other teens who have lost siblings, and in the process helps you to understand your own unique grief. She offers insights and invaluable resources to help you get through the most difficult experience and I highly recommend this book to you."

—**Carol Tosone, PhD, LCSW**, associate professor at the New York University Silver School of Social Work, and editor-in-chief of *Clinical Social Work Journal*

"This is an exquisitely written and sensitive book on a difficult and often overlooked topic. While written for teens that have suffered the loss of a sibling, the book is also of great value to parents and clinicians. The case studies and types of grieving responses make the book easily accessible to the readers."

—**Richard J. Gelles, PhD**, dean of the School of Social Policy and Practice, University of Pennsylvania

the *instant* help
solutions series

Young people today need mental health resources more than ever. That's why New Harbinger created the **Instant Help Solutions Series** especially for teens. Written by leading psychologists, physicians, and professionals, these evidence-based self-help books offer practical tips and strategies for dealing with a variety of mental health issues and life challenges teens face, such as depression, anxiety, bullying, eating disorders, trauma, and self-esteem problems.

Studies have shown that young people who learn healthy coping skills early on are better able to navigate problems later in life. Engaging and easy-to-use, these books provide teens with the tools they need to thrive—at home, at school, and on into adulthood.

This series is part of the **New Harbinger Instant Help Books** imprint, founded by renowned child psychologist Lawrence Shapiro. For a complete list of books in this series, visit newharbinger.com.

grieving for the sibling you lost

a teen's guide to coping with grief & finding meaning after loss

ERICA GOLDBLATT HYATT, DSW

Instant Help Books
An Imprint of New Harbinger Publications, Inc.

Publisher's Note

This publication is designed to provide accurate and authoritative information in regard to the subject matter covered. It is sold with the understanding that the publisher is not engaged in rendering psychological, financial, legal, or other professional services. If expert assistance or counseling is needed, the services of a competent professional should be sought.

Distributed in Canada by Raincoast Books

Copyright © 2015 by Erica Goldblatt Hyatt
                  Instant Help Books
                  An Imprint of New Harbinger Publications, Inc.
                  5674 Shattuck Avenue
                  Oakland, CA 94609
                  www.newharbinger.com

Cover design by Amy Shoup
Acquired by Melissa Valentine
Edited by Jasmine Star

Library of Congress Cataloging-in-Publication Data

Goldblatt-Hyatt, Erica.
  Grieving for the sibling you lost : a teen's guide to coping with grief and finding meaning after loss / Erica Goldblatt-Hyatt ; foreword by Kenneth Doka.
    pages cm. -- (The instant help solutions series)
  ISBN 978-1-62625-249-3 (paperback) -- ISBN (invalid) 978-1-62625-250-9 (pdf e-book) -- ISBN 978-1-62625-251-6 (epub) 1. Teenagers and death. 2. Bereavement in adolescence. 3. Grief in adolescence. I. Title.
  BF724.3.D43G65 2015
  155.9'370835--dc23

                      2015018137

Printed in the United States of America

17   16   15

10   9   8   7   6   5   4   3   2   1   First printing

For Jessica, Jake, Heide, and Mark Randall for allowing me to accompany them on their journey. For Drs. Arthur Schwartz and Tony Bruno for being my champions, on earth and from above. For my brother and sister, my partners in laughter and crime. For my loving, supportive parents, who gave me every opportunity and supported every step. For my beautiful children: our angel Darby Joss, and our rainbows Rhett Lawson and Remy Neve Beate. For my husband, William, my wonderful companion and best friend, for whom I have infinite love, respect, and admiration.

Contents

Foreword

Siblings have a unique relationship. They share a secret language—a private code that unlocks common experiences. They are family, tied together by kinship throughout life. Yet unlike most family relationships, sibling relationships are more equal and less hierarchical. Siblings also are part of each other's identity. Part of who I am and who I will always be is how I was defined while I was growing up: as Franky and Dot's kid brother.

Siblings stay important. Throughout life, we tend to share problems and seek each other's assistance and advice. And when we lose a sibling, we grieve that loss. This is true even when relationships are strained, distant, or even nonexistent. Psychologist Helen Rosen has described sibling relationships as having a number of dimensions, one of which she called closeness-distance. Some siblings are in constant contact with each other. Others seldom speak. Another dimension is warmth-hostility. Some siblings have warm, supportive relationships, whereas others argue constantly or consciously choose to limit contact. Helen Rosen noted that the more relationships veer toward either end of these continuums, the more intense the grief. So it isn't just the close, warm relationships we grieve. In fact, people often have a lot of remorse and grief about losing a sibling—even when there was conflict.

We grieve the loss of a brother or sister at any stage of life. It doesn't matter whether a sibling is nine, nineteen, or ninety years old. When a brother or sister dies, we still miss that person and grieve the loss. For teens, however, grief can be complicated. As you approach independence, it may be more difficult to reach out to the adults around you, whether parents, teachers, coaches, or clergy. You may even be reluctant to share with your friends. After all, you may want to fit in—to have an identity beyond the kid whose brother or sister died. So your grief may stay inside. In addition, as you try to work out what your own spiritual beliefs are as part of your identity, you may find your old beliefs don't fit with your new reality or offer the comfort they once did.

Whatever your situation may be, I think you'll find Erica Goldblatt Hyatt's book *Grieving for the Sibling You Lost* so helpful. It does an excellent job of describing the different ways you might experience grief. This book also offers sound advice, useful exercises, and tools for coping with your loss—and most importantly, the hope that you can do so, perhaps with support from family, friends, a counselor, or other trusted adults.

Ultimately, *Grieving for the Sibling You Lost* will help you acknowledge and recognize your loss and grief—something we all need to do when we lose a loved one. You've lost a critical part of your identity. You've lost someone who may have shared your deepest and earliest memories, who probably knew all of your nicknames, and who may have been among your closest friends. In these pages, you'll find support in honoring your brother or sister, adapting to your loss, and even finding meaning in it.

—Kenneth J. Doka, PhD
Professor, Graduate School,
The College of New Rochelle
Senior Consultant,
The Hospice Foundation of America

Acknowledgments

Thank you to Jasoleil Amber Cineus, former student, now friend and peer, who was a terrific assistant during the editing process.

I am indebted to Melissa Valentine and New Harbinger Publications for recognizing the value of this book, and for reaching out to me to get it written.

Finally, I must acknowledge the brilliant editing of Jasmine Star, who was a delight to work with and helped make my words all the more authentic and accessible.

Introduction

I'm a professor now, but I used to be a social worker. I felt called to do the work many people shy away from—in the field of death and dying, helping both adults and children facing terminal illness. It wasn't easy, but I loved it and have retained a passion for the area to this very day. I believe that while I may play a small role in each person's life journey, the patients and families I've worked with have left a far greater mark on me. One family touched me so deeply and changed my life so profoundly that they inspired the book you hold in your hands.

I met Wren, a lovely fifteen-year-old with a rare form of leukemia, when I was a pediatric oncology social worker at the hospital where she received her treatment. Although Wren's father, Jackson, claimed his daughter was an ordinary teenager, from the moment I met her I felt otherwise. My first impression of Wren was of a soft-spoken, sweet girl with an artistic and eclectic sense of style; even when she was feeling at her worst, she wore cowboy boots, and when radiation left her with a bald spot and thinned her hair, she shaved it into a Mohawk. Still, Wren was like most teenagers in many ways: she liked coloring her hair, writing poetry, and spending time with her pets. She'd send her boyfriend secret videos of herself silently dancing in the bathroom after her family had fallen asleep. She was funny, compassionate, and bright. But beneath the surface of all that, Wren was an old soul, a deeply spiritual and special young woman.

Wren was quiet and we never spoke much, but she caught my attention because of her love of poetry. I gave her a book of love poems by my favorite author, Pablo Neruda, and I felt deeply connected to her in ways I still cannot explain. Perhaps I saw so much of myself in her as she searched for meaning, delving into the works of poets and scholars who pondered love and death. In my office at the college where I work today, I still have a framed lithograph of her poetry and art by my desk.

Wren bravely battled cancer for two years before losing her life shortly after she turned seventeen. I'll never forget the morning I read about Wren's death in the online journal her father used to keep Wren's fans informed about how she was doing. I was sitting at a friend's cottage on a beautiful, peaceful day. My heart sank and I felt sick to my stomach, knowing the world had lost a special person. I wondered how everything could simultaneously feel so beautiful, with birds chirping around me and a gentle breeze blowing through the window, and yet so hollow without Wren. I felt as though time should stop and the world should stand still—life simply couldn't be the same. Driving home, I cried and just existed in the sadness of the day, wondering where Wren was now and what she was doing. She's still very much a living presence in my life.

Soon after Wren's death, something unexpected emerged from her story: the healing process her younger sister, Amaya, went through. Amaya was mostly at school when Wren was in the hospital, and like her sister, she was quiet, so I didn't speak with her much. But I sometimes saw her at the hospital and, later, at memorial events for her sister. In the aftermath of losing Wren,

I spent a lot of time talking with Jackson about how Amaya was coping with losing her sister. Though I didn't know Amaya very well, I knew the death of such a close sibling would be hard. Amaya went through a very difficult time, and as Jackson and his wife, Lindsay, continued to reach out to me for advice and support, I looked for resources to help Amaya cope.

I was shocked when I couldn't find anything for her. No self-help book was available for a teen grieving the loss of a brother or sister. In fact, there was no book on this topic for anyone: parents, teachers, therapists, or professors. I couldn't believe it. Yet day in, day out, teens are experiencing the death of a sibling. To add to this, teens are much more aware of death than adults give them credit for. In fact, awareness of death begins in childhood. I recall my five-year-old nephew telling me once, out of the blue, "Every day, people are dying."

Loss is hard for everyone, and also different for everyone. The loss of a sibling during adolescence can shake your sense of self just as it's beginning to develop. Siblings are our partners and rivals, our first friends, and our first enemies. Being a teenager is hard enough without having to cope with this kind of loss. It's a time when your whole life is changing and your world is opening up as you start creating some distance from your family and begin to ask yourself, *Who am I?*

If you're a teenager and you've lost a brother or sister, this book is for you. You may be feeling fine, you may be hurting badly, or you may find yourself somewhere in between. Wherever you are, it's okay to be there. My hope is that, in the pages of this book, you'll see that others are going through what you are—even though there's no one else exactly like you in the world. This book is a safe place for you; it will help guide you through your grief, teach you ways to cope, and explore ways you can memorialize your brother or sister. It will also help you adjust to your new "normal"—life without your sibling. In these pages, I offer you space to cry, reflect, celebrate, and find some meaning in your loss.

There are many valuable messages for you in this book, but one of the most important is this: how you cope doesn't have to turn into who you are. You aren't alone; you don't have to struggle by yourself. And although coping with grief is hard, there are ways to do it.

Part 1 of this book offers an introduction to grief, grieving, and how a brother or sister's death can affect your understanding of who you are. In part 2, you'll learn about different coping styles that are common among teens who lose a sibling. Finally, in part 3, you'll learn many specific techniques that will help you in your journey toward healing. You don't need to read this book in order. Each chapter is meant to stand alone so that you can learn at your own pace, in whatever way works best for you. My hope is that, eventually, you'll work through the entire book, but only when the time is right for you. One word of advice: Keep a journal or paper and pencil handy for doing the exercises, and so you can jot down ideas that come to you as you read. (Just to keep things simple, in the book I'll usually say "journal," but you can use any kind of notebook or just separate sheets of paper for the exercises.)

This book is Wren's legacy to me and her gift to you. I hope you find it helpful.

Part 1

Grief, Grieving, and Being a Teen

chapter 1

Grief

In this chapter, I provide a brief overview of what grief is. Since it's sometimes easier to learn from examples than descriptions, let's take a look at three different teenagers who lost a sibling and what their experience of grief was like.

✳ William

William is fifteen. His brother, Michael, died four months ago at the age of seventeen. Ever since Michael died, William hasn't felt like himself. For one thing, he notices that he feels very tired, even from the moment he wakes up in the morning. "I have to try really hard to get out of bed," William says. "I feel like I didn't get a good night's sleep, even if I went to bed early. Sometimes the earlier I go to bed, the more I wake up in the middle of the night, and sometimes I just totally pass out and don't wake up until my alarm goes off, but I still feel like I didn't get enough sleep." William's mother keeps asking him if he feels depressed, but he doesn't notice feeling sad. In fact, he feels abnormal because he hasn't cried over the loss of his brother. He misses Michael a lot and thinks about him frequently, but he hasn't been able to cry. He says, "I worry that my mom thinks I didn't care about Michael, but that couldn't be further from the truth. It's just that I feel so empty about the whole thing."

William and Michael used to spend lots of time together, especially playing soccer and basketball. Now that Michael is gone, William doesn't have any interest in playing sports. His body feels both hollow and heavy at the same time. His joints feel achy, he's rarely hungry, and sometimes he feels as though he's in a daze. William has difficulty finding the words to explain how he's feeling in his body. He just feels different, and he's afraid that things will never be normal again.

✱ Ariel

Ariel is fourteen years old. Her sister, Myra, died a year ago at age eight when she hit her head after a fall on some playground equipment, passed out an hour later, and never woke up. Ariel is just starting high school, and she fears leaving the house in the morning to go to school because she worries that something bad might happen to her. Ariel says, "Nobody thought Myra was going to die. It happened out of nowhere, and since then, I feel scared that I'm going to die all of a sudden too." Ariel no longer feels safe. To her, it seems like her parents are paying extra close attention to her, and she worries about what would happen to them if she were to die too. In addition, Ariel thinks that because she was the older sister, she somehow let her parents down when Myra died. She feels guilty for not doing a better job of protecting her.

During the day, Ariel tries her best to be brave and smile when she interacts with teachers and friends, but at home she cries frequently and feels sad and lonely, even when she's surrounded by family members. Ariel thinks about Myra a lot and wonders if she felt any pain when she died. Ariel also says, "I never really thought about dying, and now I can't stop thinking about it. I want to ask my mom and dad questions, but they're already upset, so there really isn't anybody around to talk to about this stuff." Like William, she worries that this is her "new normal," that she'll feel sad and alone forever. And given that it's been a year since Myra died, Ariel wonders if she should be doing better. What makes her feel even worse is that there are times when she's so angry at Myra for dying that she can't focus on anything else. Yet there are other times when she's doing something, such as homework, and doesn't think about Myra at all. Ariel feels very confused. Ariel doesn't know what to think, what to say, and how to act in this new life without her sister.

✳ Jordan

Jordan's older sister, Emily, died eight years ago. Jordan is now sixteen years old. He's remembering less and less about his big sister, and that makes him feel guilty. Emily died of a very long illness, so she wasn't home very much in the last year of her life. Jordan feels he never really got the chance to get to know who Emily was outside of being his sick sister. What he does remember about Emily is that she was frequently hospitalized and that his parents often left him with his grandmother so that they could be with her. Jordan says, "I spent a lot of time with my grandmother from the age of six to eight. She was lots of fun and I really felt like she was my mom. I was always excited to go to her house because when I was with Grammy, she went *out of her way to make sure I was having a good time. It was so different when I was at home with my parents. If Emily was home, they bent over backward caring for her. If she was in the hospital, they spent all their time talking about going to see Emily, calling her doctors, or arguing about her treatment. They expected me to shut up and be good. There was never any time when it was just about me."*

When Jordan looks back on all of that, he feels resentful. As a child, he watched the world revolve around Emily, and he feels he hardly had any chances to make happy memories with his family. He says, "I missed out on things like having a mom and dad who took me to baseball games or showed up for parent-teacher meetings. Of course they loved me, but they just weren't around." Even after all these years, he feels forgotten, as though Emily is still more important than him. His parents continue to talk about Emily as if she's alive, and Jordan worries that they'll never get over losing her. He also feels that they don't understand him and, what's worse, that they don't seem to try to. And because of their focus on Emily, Jordan says he feels bad about himself, as though he doesn't matter. He doesn't speak to his parents much anymore and prefers to spend time with his friends. Yet even when he's happy, he feels uncomfortable, as though it isn't appropriate to feel good.

What Is Grief?

William, Ariel, and Jordan are all experiencing symptoms of grief after the loss of a brother or sister. And as you may have noticed, each of them is feeling, thinking, and acting differently after losing a sibling. It's important to know that while each teen grieves differently, everyone's grief is very real.

"Grief" can be defined as a collection of feelings that result from the death of somebody important in your life. Grief can take many forms and is different for each person. The process of experiencing grief, also called grieving, can have many effects, mostly in three main areas:

* Your physical body

* Your emotions and thoughts

* How you relate to others

The experience of grief actually has symptoms, just like a cold or virus does. It's common for people to fear that grieving means they're "going crazy" and something is wrong with them, but grief is almost always a natural process that people go through when they lose someone they love.

Years ago, people used to think that it was important to "get over" the loss of a brother or sister. Therapists, teachers, friends, and family members might have encouraged teens to "move on" and "deal with" death. These days, most people understand that grieving doesn't mean forgetting about your sibling and moving on; rather, it means learning how to live your life without an important person in it. It means taking your time and finding ways to cope with the loss that work for you, and maybe even finding some meaning in your loss. This can be hard, especially because people tend to have complex relationships with their siblings. Perhaps you fought frequently, or maybe there were times when you felt jealous of your brother or sister. Maybe the two of you were closer when you were younger, but as you became a teenager, you found that you didn't have much in common with your brother or sister anymore. Maybe your sibling was younger and you felt like a parent to him or her, or maybe your sibling was older and felt like the parent to you. Relationships are unique, so grieving your sibling will be a unique process. No two people grieve the same way.

Exercise: Describing Your Experience

Before beginning the next chapter, ask yourself whether you're grieving, even if you're not sure of the answer to this question right now. Then, in your journal on a piece of paper, or using the worksheet available for download at http://www.newharbinger.com/32493—see the very back of this book for download instructions—jot down a few of your personal experiences related to losing your brother or sister, perhaps a summary similar to those for William, Ariel, and Jordan. Then, as you read on, you can refer back to what you wrote to see what it can tell you about your own grief process.

Concluding Thoughts

It's important to learn about the process and symptoms of grief. And if you've been judging yourself, try to let that go. Grief is a painful and difficult process—and one that's different for each individual. Whatever you feel is fine. That's your experience. By looking at your experience and understanding it better, you can facilitate the process of healing, without losing sight of how important your brother or sister was to you and will always be.

chapter 2

Symptoms of Grief

Grieving can feel like work, and you may even sometimes hear it called "grief work." This is because the process of coping with loss can be physically and mentally exhausting. Some teens start feeling the effects of grief from the moment they learn that their brother or sister has died. For others it takes some time to sink in, and they may even feel numb.

Physical Symptoms

If you think back on William, in chapter 1, he primarily felt grief in his physical body. He was surprised that he didn't cry after his brother died; in fact, he felt like there might be something wrong with him because he didn't. William's body appeared to react to Michael's death first. William may not have known it, but he was doing grief work as his body struggled to adjust to the lack of his brother's presence in his life. Since William was accustomed to spending time with his brother being active and playing sports, it isn't surprising that he experienced physical symptoms of grief.

Losing a brother or sister is a physical event: you lose somebody who you thought would always be there. And your body may be grieving even if you aren't aware of it. Plus, physical symptoms might make it harder for you to focus your emotions or what you're thinking. Here are some of the most common physical symptoms of grief, with quotes from teens about their experiences with them. Have you ever felt any of these symptoms?

* Loss of appetite or changes in eating habits.

  Mary, nineteen: "I just don't feel hungry anymore, and I don't enjoy eating. When I try to eat, food just sits in my stomach, and it feels uncomfortable."

* Insomnia and sleep disturbances

  Ron, fourteen: "I have a hard time going to sleep at night. My body feels so awake, like I drank a big energy drink. When I do fall asleep, I wake up every few hours."

* Getting sick often

  Janina, fifteen: "I've stayed home from school this year more than ever before. I always seem to have a cold or stomach bug. My body feels like it's shutting down on me."

* Loss of energy

  Terrance, eighteen: "I'm so tired all the time. My body feels heavy, like I have weights strapped to my back."

* Stomachaches

  Martha, thirteen: "My tummy hurts all the time. It feels tight and crampy, like I ate something bad."

✱ Headaches

Jin, seventeen: "I never had bad headaches before. Now I have at least one per day. Lights feel brighter, and it feels like my head is caught in a vise. My mom says I'm being dramatic."

✱ Achy joints

Brandon, fourteen: "I joke that I'm an old man now. When I wake up in the morning, everything feels tight and stiff, almost like I have the flu."

✱ Muscle tension

Brynna, eighteen: "I clench my jaw so tightly now, and sometimes I don't even realize it until a friend tells me I'm making a face. I grind my teeth and even clench my fists most of the time."

✱ Ulcers

Diana, sixteen: "I was diagnosed with a bleeding ulcer. That's something mostly older people get, when there's a little break in your stomach that causes bleeding. They say it happens from stress."

✱ Body pain

Jose, fifteen: "I hurt all the time, all over. It doesn't matter where—my body just feels sore."

* Asthma or trouble breathing

  Martin, thirteen: "There are times when I can't get a deep enough breath. It scares me, and my doctor said that when I get scared, that makes it even harder to breathe."

* Bed-wetting

  Reuben, fourteen: "This is really embarrassing—I stopped wetting the bed when I was a little kid, but now it's happening again. I have no control over it."

* Feeling dazed

  Michelle, eighteen: "It feels like I'm looking out from behind a mask—like I'm not quite myself. It's hard to explain, but I feel separated from my body."

* Feeling physically off or out of sync

  Anna, eighteen: "Sometimes I feel like I'm floating or dizzy—like I'm a step behind everyone else and always trying to catch up. That's so not me. Usually I'm ahead of everyone."

* Physical symptoms similar to those of your sibling

  Allen, nineteen: "My brother died of a brain tumor. When he was first diagnosed, he had trouble finding the right words to say what he wanted to say. Sometimes I have trouble finding words or say the wrong thing. I worry it means I have a brain tumor too."

✱ Fearing that physical symptoms mean death is coming

Arriana, seventeen: "I have lots of weird things happening in my body now—random aches and pains and just feeling uncomfortable. It makes me worry that I might not wake up in the morning, like I might die in my sleep."

Maybe you can relate to some of the physical symptoms above, or maybe you've experienced others that aren't on the list. It might be helpful for you to write any physical symptoms you're experiencing in your journal, or on the worksheet available for download at http://www.newharbinger.com/32493.

Psychological Symptoms

Let's return to the three stories at the beginning of chapter 1. While William's grief was very physical in nature, both Ariel and Jordan were experiencing more psychological symptoms of grief. You may be more familiar with symptoms like Ariel's and Jordan's, since adults may feel more comfortable asking you questions like "How are you doing?" or telling you about their emotions or what they're thinking about.

Symptoms that involve thoughts or emotions can all be called psychological. For example, Ariel's understanding of what it means to live a safe and protected life has been changed by her sister's death. In addition to fearing something bad might happen to her, she also experiences intense emotions, including sadness and worry. Jordan, on the other hand, feels less confident about himself and even feels abandoned by his parents.

Ariel and Jordan are grieving normally, but in a different way than William, whose grief is also normal. Here are some of the most common psychological symptoms of grief, again with a quote from a teen for each one. Have you ever felt any of these symptoms?

* Difficulty with concentration

   Alyssa, thirteen: "My teachers are always telling me to pay more attention in class, but I can't. There are so many thoughts on my mind now."

* Feeling powerless or helpless

   Ellen, eighteen: "I feel like it doesn't matter what I say or do. Life is out of my control. I could die any minute, so it's hard to really feel good."

* Restlessness

   Alexander, fifteen: "I'm shifting around all the time and jittery in both my body and my mind. I feel trapped, like I'm in a cage or being smothered in some way."

* Fear of dying or fear of dying at the same age as your sibling

   Reina, sixteen: "My sister died when she was seventeen. I'll be seventeen in three months, and I kind of feel like I have three months left to live. I'm not sick, and I know that doesn't make sense, but it's how I feel."

✳ Fear of the dark

Duane, fourteen: "I never slept with a nightlight before, but now when it's dark, I feel alone and scared, like something bad is going to happen. If I leave even a small light on when I go to bed, that helps me feel better."

✳ Fear of getting close to others

Katherina, sixteen: "Why bother having a relationship with anyone if we're all going to die one day? It hurts too much to say good-bye. I've started spending less time with my friends because I wasn't ready when my brother died. I need to be ready if someone else dies."

✳ Wishing for death

Ben, thirteen: "Sometimes I wish I were dead. I'm not suicidal and I'm not going to kill myself, but it seems easier to be gone than to stay here and feel all the pain."

✳ Fear of "going crazy"

Elena, nineteen: "I honestly feel like I'm losing my mind because of all my racing thoughts, sadness, and feeling so alone. I worry that I'm going insane."

* Feeling like a burden

  Sarah, thirteen: "I feel like my parents don't want me around and like they don't want to take care of me. They have too much going on. I take up too much of their time."

* Feeling dangerous to others

  Bryan, seventeen: "I tell people, 'You don't want to get to know me. I'm bad luck. The people I love seem to up and die, so it's not worth it.'"

* New fears

  Phoebe, fifteen: "I'm afraid of everything now— afraid I might drown when I'm in the water, afraid of being in a plane crash, afraid of suffocating while I sleep. I used to be bold, but now I'm so afraid of something going wrong."

* Nightmares

  James, thirteen: "I have bad dreams almost every night. They don't make sense and I don't always remember them, but I wake up with a feeling like something bad is going to happen."

* Low self-esteem

  Preston, sixteen: "I have a lot to feel confident about: I'm a football player and I do great in school. So I can't understand why I just feel so lame, ugly, and useless."

* Feeling uncomfortable when happy

  Maren, eighteen: "I had a really good day yesterday. The sun was shining, and I was spending time with my friends just feeling good. Then I got this sinking feeling, like it was wrong to feel happy. My sister is dead, and she can't feel anything anymore, so I shouldn't be allowed to feel happy either."

* Feeling overprotected by parents

  Lincoln, fifteen: "My parents don't let me go out with friends anymore. They keep me in the house. They monitor everything I do like I'm a prisoner."

* Feeling underprotected by parents

  Trent, fifteen: "My parents don't seem to care where I go or what I do. I could stay out all night, and they wouldn't notice I was gone."

* Feeling lonely

  Bethany, nineteen: "I can be in a room with family and friends and still feel completely alone. I feel like nobody understands what I'm going through, and maybe nobody cares."

* Feeling more symptoms during the holidays

  Caspar, eighteen: "At Christmastime I feel more depressed. Even though it's been seven years since my brother died, I just notice his absence more when we're gathered around the table and he's so obviously missing. That makes me really sad."

✱ Believing your parents may never be the same

Christina, fourteen: "I seriously doubt my mom will ever be happy again. She's lost her smile, and it just seems like every day is so hard for her."

As with physical symptoms, perhaps you recognize some of the psychological symptoms listed above, or maybe you've experienced others. It might be helpful for you to write any psychological symptoms you're experiencing in your journal or on the worksheet available online.

Psychological symptoms can be hard to get past because your thoughts and feelings have an effect on each other. For example, if you're feeling lonely, you might tell yourself, *I'll feel lonely forever. I'll always be alone.* This is a very normal thought that comes from the grief process, yet it can cause you to feel sad and stuck for a very long time. Part 3 of this book offers some techniques for working with thoughts to help you move forward in your grief process.

Behavioral Symptoms

Now let's revisit Jordan's story, which provides some clear behavioral symptoms of grief. Behavioral symptoms are things that show up in how we act in our daily lives. They may be behaviors you choose to do, like skipping school, or they may be things you aren't necessarily aware of, like staying away from other people because social interactions feel draining.

Jordan has many difficult thoughts and feelings on the inside, and he also has changes on the outside since Emily died—changes in how he acts toward his parents and others in his life. Jordan's situation is difficult. Although he's trying to spend more time with his friends, he may feel different around them. And his friends may not treat him the same way they did before Emily died. Plus, he may feel uncomfortable showing his sadness or frustration to his friends out of fear that they'll treat him differently. As a result, Jordan may not behave as he would if he were expressing his natural grieving process. Here are some of the most common behavioral symptoms of grief, again with examples provided by teens I've worked with:

* Increased aggression or hostility toward others and picking fights

   Jack, fifteen: "I definitely am becoming a bully. I don't even know why, but I'm picking fights with people who can't fight back. Weak kids at school make me angry."

* Getting involved in risky behaviors like drinking or taking drugs

   Gemma, eighteen: "I used to be pretty good, but I've had more of a wild side recently. I've been going to more parties, and I've been drinking a lot. I've been keeping it a secret from my parents because I know they wouldn't approve, and even my friends tell me I'm getting too drunk for my own good."

* Acting out in class

   Abigail, sixteen: "I'm the class clown. If I can get a laugh out of one of my friends, I'll do anything. My homeroom teacher has a problem with that because she says it's distracting."

* Rebelling against your parents

  Bryden, thirteen: "I fight with my parents all the time. If they tell me to do something, I don't do it or I do the opposite. I haven't cleaned my room or done my chores in three weeks."

* Becoming more secretive

  Khalil, fifteen: "I'm like a safe you can't crack. I don't tell anyone anything about myself, especially parents and teachers. People ask me lots of questions about how I'm feeling, what my plans are for after high school, or what I'm doing this summer, and I don't tell them anything."

Just as with physical and psychological symptoms, there may be other behavioral symptoms of grief that I haven't listed here. Consider this list to be more of a discussion starter than something all-inclusive. It might be helpful for you to write about any behavioral symptoms you're experiencing on the worksheet available at the website for this book, or in your journal.

Symptoms: Something Added or Something Taken Away

If you look over the lists above, you might notice that symptoms of grief can take two different forms: thoughts, feelings, and behaviors can be either added or taken away from your life, like pluses and minuses. For example, Ariel has symptoms that didn't exist until after her sister died, such as feeling unsafe. A new feeling has been added to her life. On the other hand, Jordan is feeling a loss of confidence, so confidence has been subtracted from his life. The next exercise will help you think about your grief symptoms in terms of pluses (+) for things that have been added and minuses (–) for things that have been taken away.

Exercise: Identifying Your Own Pluses and Minuses

It can be helpful to recognize how life has changed since your brother or sister died by looking at the addition and subtraction of thoughts, feelings, and behaviors. You can use the worksheet available at http://www .newharbinger.com/32493 to complete this activity; or, in your journal, write two headings: "Plus Symptoms (+)" and "Minus Symptoms (–)." Then take some time to list new thoughts, feelings, or behaviors that have come up since the death of your sibling under "Plus Symptoms." Beneath "Minus Symptoms," list any thoughts, feelings, or behaviors that are missing now. If you feel uncertain about which symptoms fall into which category, the examples below may help.

Plus Symptoms (+)

- Example: *I cry way more than before.*

- Example: *I feel nauseated and like I'm going to throw up when I look at food.*

Minus Symptoms (–)

- Example: *I'm losing sleep at night.*

- Example: *I feel like I care less about my friends and their problems.*

Writing out your positive and negative symptoms and reviewing them is a good first step toward getting a fuller picture of how you're feeling in the aftermath of your sibling's death.

How Parents and Caregivers Grieve

There are many books devoted entirely to the topic of parents or caregivers grieving a lost child. Since this book is focused on teens, here I'll just highlight a few common responses that you might notice in the adults in your family. Parents and caregivers also grieve, and they experience both positive and negative symptoms. And like teens, no two parents or caregivers are the same. You may be living with both of your parents, or you may have only one parent in your life. Your parents may be heterosexual, or they may be same-sex. You could be spending time with or even living with a grandmother, grandfather, or other extended family member. The adults in your life all had different relationships with your sibling than you did.

The lists below are nowhere near exhaustive, but they do highlight a few symptoms you may see in your parents or caregivers, with a focus on symptoms that may affect you:

Plus Symptoms (+)

* Crying

* Raising their voices or yelling at you or others

* Having increased expectations of you or others

* Being angry or irritable

* Showing high energy and never slowing down

* Jumping from topic to topic during conversation and not wanting to talk deeply about things

Minus Symptoms (−)

* Withdrawing from family-based events, such as dinners, birthday celebrations, or getting together for the holidays

* Seeming to lack emotion

* Not being very present in your life

* Not communicating much

* Not seeming interested in the world or other people

* Not being on time for important appointments

* Forgetting details about you or others, including neglecting routine tasks like preparing meals or picking you up from school

Adults who are grieving often don't realize how their symptoms are affecting their children. They may be so focused on their own feelings that they don't realize that their words or actions may sometimes be hurtful. Understand that they truly don't intend to hurt you. Still, you may find yourself in a very tough situation: you've lost a sibling, and now you may feel like you've lost a parent or caregiver too. You may feel very lonely. I hope that the examples above will help you see that your parents or caregivers are also doing grief work. But because of their own difficulties, they may not be able to attend to your feelings. In this book, I want to honor your feelings and help you find ways to work with them. I also provide an information sheet you might give to a parent or adult who's struggling with grief that might help him or her deal with feelings and the grief work he or she is doing; you can download it at the website for this book, http://www.newharbinger.com/32493.

That said, here's one final and important note: Some teens may feel like they have to take care of their parents or other caregivers as they grieve. It's good to be sensitive to their feelings and provide whatever support you can, but you also need to express your own grief and receive support. Please be sure to remember that you are not responsible for the adults in your life. Despite their grief, they are still in charge. You can't be their therapist or friend, and you can't parent them. Adults need to find resources to support them in their own grief processes, just like you're doing by working with this book.

How Teen Grief Is Special

As a teen, you're in a special place with your grief. You don't need to rely only on your parents or caregivers to take care of all your needs, and you're starting to become independent. You're starting to look outward, to friends, mentors, teachers, and other role models, to better understand yourself and the world around you. At the same time, it's important to have supportive family members to guide you in your journey.

One thing that makes grieving such a challenge is that it can be hard to figure out who you are when a piece of your family puzzle is missing. Siblings help us learn healthy boundaries and family rules, and they give us an opportunity to explore close relationships. Losing your sibling may feel like losing a piece of yourself. Yet because your family members are also grieving, they may be less present to help provide support as you try to become the new you, after your loss.

Also, during adolescence, many parts of you are in flux, including your brain. Aside from when you were first born, this is the time in your life when your brain is changing the most. Your hormones are fluctuating, causing changes and growth spurts in your body and impacting your thoughts and feelings. Even aside from grief, these changes can be challenging or confusing. You may feel like you need an outlet for expressing yourself, and this may drive you to try more risky activities, yet you may push yourself too far. It can be hard to keep yourself safe when your body and brain are changing so much, and it can be hard to make sound decisions if hormones are influencing you. Add grief to the mix, and you may be more likely to try drugs, to drink, or to take part in risky activities that get your blood pumping, like shoplifting or hanging out in unsafe neighborhoods.

Grief Is Cyclical

The process of grieving is often cyclical, changing depending on the day and whatever else is happening in your life. For example, during the holidays your grief symptoms might feel very strong because this is usually a time when families get together, which may make it obvious that a member of your family is absent. As a result, you may feel sad, irritable, or overwhelmed. Other times, your symptoms of grief may be fewer or less intense, or they may be entirely absent. If you're distracted by homework, friends, or work responsibilities, you may even forget that you're grieving. When this happens, sometimes people feel guilty because they think they should be grieving their loved one all the time.

Also, it's important to understand that grief doesn't exist in a vacuum. Your life includes many different activities, relationships, issues, and other factors that make you uniquely you. Throughout, the loss of your brother or sister might come up at different times and in different places. This can happen in both expected and unexpected ways. You may be caught off guard by sadness, anxiety, or other symptoms when you take part in activities your sibling used to do or go to places that you visited together or as a family. Part of grief work is understanding the cyclical nature of grief and coping with different feelings, or even the absence of feelings, at different times.

Grief Is Like a Big Wave with a Strong Undertow

Imagine a surfer facing a big wave cresting toward him. It's fierce and knocks him off his board, and a strong undertow drags him beneath the surface of the water. Grief symptoms are similar: like strong and often overpowering waves that can knock you down, allowing the undertow to pull you below. These waves may come when you least expect it.

Now, returning to our surfer, what does he do when he's knocked down and pulled under? One response may be to panic and struggle, fighting the strong undercurrent and believing he can overcome it. Yet he only exhausts himself in his struggle to swim back to the shore. It's inevitable that he'll be pulled out to sea, because he's no match for the power of the currents and waves. Again, this is like grief: symptoms can be sudden, powerful, and stronger than you expect, even if they've been brewing for a while. When you're hit by waves of grief, it's common to feel like you need to fight. You might do this by ignoring your symptoms as you try to push through and get on with life, thinking you can handle everything on your own.

It might be more helpful to take a lesson from an accomplished surfer, who instead of struggling to swim against the current, relaxes and allows the water to carry him. He may float on top of the waves or even swim beside them. He understands that if he keeps struggling against the undercurrent, he'll become exhausted and may even drown. As he acknowledges the power and strength of the current, works with it, and goes with the waves, the undertow will eventually weaken, allowing him to swim safely to shore. So if you can, go with your symptoms of grief, stopping the fight, letting them happen, and working to understand them, just like surfing in tempestuous seas. Eventually you can get back to the safety of the shore.

Of course, it isn't easy to let go and stop fighting. People tend to try to push through hard times. Sometimes, however, the best approach is to let your symptoms be, experiencing them and learning what they're trying to tell you. You might find it helpful to write about any waves of grief you're experiencing, using the worksheet available at http://www.newhar binger.com/32493 or your journal.

Concluding Thoughts

Grief can come at you like strong waves that drag you under, but your symptoms may also be like the quieter, more consistent ripples at the shore. Yet even quiet ripples can have big effects. They can eventually cause the sand of the beach to be swept back into the sea or grind down the shells and driftwood in their path. Take some time to consider your own symptoms. Do they show up only occasionally, but in a big way, knocking you over and leaving you gasping for air? Or are they ever-present, eating away at your life, friendships, and plans for the future? However it manifests, grief can be life changing, but it isn't always for the worse. As you work your way through this book, you'll have many opportunities to explore your experience. You may discover that your symptoms have taught you deep and meaningful lessons about who you are.

chapter 3

Understanding Your Grief

If you've recognized some of your symptoms or some of what you're going through in this book so far, that probably means you're grieving. But if you feel as though you can't relate to the material in chapters 1 and 2, don't worry. As mentioned, grieving is a uniquely personal experience, and no two teens will grieve the loss of a sibling in the same way. There has never been anybody exactly like you in the world, and this may be your first experience with loss, so it may take some time for you to get to know your own style of grieving. There's room for everybody's personal way of working with loss, even if that style is unusual or unique. And no matter what your experience, understand that grieving doesn't mean you're mentally ill or indicate that there's something wrong with you. It just means you're experiencing a new and painful phase of your life. That can be quite an adjustment.

When to Seek Professional Help

Contrary to popular belief, grief is rarely dangerous, even though it can cause some very intense feelings. Still, it's important to understand when you might need some professional help. So let's imagine a scale of grief intensity ranging from 0 to 100. The closer you are to 0, the milder your symptoms are. The closer you are to 100, the more intense they are. Below, I'm going to outline a few basic symptoms on the scale that you may relate to. Keep in mind that because grief is like waves that ebb and flow, some days you may feel like you're more toward the lower end of the scale, and some days you may feel as though you're at the top. This is completely natural.

0 to 25: If your grief is on the lower end of the spectrum, you may feel few or no symptoms. Some time may have passed since you lost your sibling, and you may feel as though you've learned to incorporate the death of your brother or sister into your life. On the other hand, if you think your rating is 0, you may feel uncomfortable, wondering if something is wrong with you. There can be various reasons for such a low rating. One reason, especially if your loss is recent, is being in shock, meaning that although you probably aren't even aware of it, your body is trying to protect you from feeling the pain of your loss. This is like what happens when people experience a sudden physical injury: They don't always feel the pain right away because their bodies go into survival mode and surge with powerful chemicals like the stress hormone adrenaline, allowing them to get the help they need. In the same way, it might simply be too painful to realize that you've lost someone so important to you. Having a very low rating may also indicate denial, meaning not wanting to delve into what life will look like without your sibling and what your loss means. Denial is actually fairly common. Sometimes it's easier to cope by pretending life hasn't changed.

25 to 50: If your grief is generally in the range of 25 to 50, you may be experiencing a few symptoms, both plus (something added to your life) and minus (something subtracted from your life). You may think about your sibling frequently, and you may be doing some grief work that distracts you a bit from life as you used to know it. There may be times when you feel sadder or lonelier, and other times when you feel relatively comfortable. You may feel as though you're coping well for the most part, but certain triggers, like your sibling's favorite song or a movie you wish you could see together, might make some days harder than others.

50 to 75: If you're more often in the range of 50 to 75, your symptoms are more intense. They may take up more of your daily life, to the point where there are days when you really find yourself struggling. You may not always have the words for your grief, and you may wonder if this type of grieving is normal. You may worry about going crazy. Or, you may feel so empty inside that you're also concerned that things aren't right.

75 to 100: Finally, if you're at 75 to 100 on the spectrum, you're probably having a great deal of difficulty focusing on living your life in the moment. You may feel very depressed and confused, and you may be hurting deeply. Your grief may be affecting how you relate to others, perhaps making it hard to connect with friends and family. You may feel as though things will never get better and worry about life never being the same. Overall, you're probably having trouble just functioning from day to day, and aspects of life that used to be enjoyable for you may not be at all fun anymore. You may even avoid pleasurable activities because you feel you don't deserve to be happy.

It may be helpful to think about your own grief as it lies on the scale; a worksheet for this is available at http://www .newharbinger.com/32493. If you're spending a lot of time at the low end of the range (0 to 25), don't judge yourself too harshly. Go with the wave of symptoms, even if it feels confusing or unnatural. You may not have such a low rating forever, or you may learn to feel more comfortable with being on the lower end of the scale.

However, if you're spending a lot of time in the high range and feel as though there's never a break in your symptoms, it would be a good idea to talk to a trusted adult, like a teacher, clergyperson, or school counselor. Sometimes interacting with a caring professional can be enough to help you start feeling better. You may not need long-term therapy, but there can be tremendous value in knowing that somebody wants to hear about more about your journey through grief.

If you're thinking about hurting yourself—whether ending your life or cutting, burning, or hitting your body to express your emotional pain—it's important to seek help right away. Please know that there is no shame in asking for help. It's actually one of the bravest steps you can take.

It's very rare, but sometimes siblings can feel so hopeless and helpless that they consider suicide. If you feel as though no adults in your life are available for you or feel uncomfortable talking to them about suicide, call the National Suicide Prevention Lifeline: 1-800-273-8255 (TALK). You can also visit their website (http://www.suicidepreventionlifeline.org) and chat online. You'll find someone willing to listen and connect with you twenty-four hours a day, seven days a week. The staff at the hotline can connect you with a support group and help you create a safety plan and learn what to do next. If you aren't sure what to say when you call, just explain your situation: "My sibling died and I've been feeling very depressed and down. I think I might hurt myself and I need some help." Remember, it's a sign of strength to ask for help when you need it.

If you're thinking about hurting someone else, also please reach out and ask for help. Taking the first step can feel frightening, but learning how to ask for help now will benefit you in the long run.

Understanding What PTSD Is and Whether You Have It

You may have heard about post-traumatic stress disorder (PTSD) in relation to soldiers returning from combat with troublesome symptoms. But did you know that PTSD can affect anybody who has experienced a trauma? "Trauma" can be defined as an intense event that makes a person feel as though her well-being, whether emotional or physical, has been threatened. Traumatic events are unusual and out of the ordinary and may cause the person to feel horror, hopelessness, intense fear, or other distressing emotions. When people go through a trauma, their bodies react: their heart rate increases, they may sweat, their stomach may feel upset, and they may experience terror and frightening thoughts, such as *I'm going to die.*

Sometimes a sibling's death can be traumatic. If you watched your sibling die or heard details about his or her death that were upsetting, and these experiences had the effects listed above, this could be considered a trauma for you. In other words, you may be traumatized. After a trauma, people often have trouble getting the event out of their mind. They may think about it constantly, feel unsafe, and even have nightmares about it. Over time, this initial reaction to the trauma may ease, but there's also a chance that it won't go away. Here are some symptoms traumatized people may experience over the long haul:

* **Repeatedly experiencing the trauma.** Events and details of the trauma may play over and over again in their mind, sometimes in the form of nightmares, and sometimes in the form of flashbacks during the day. During flashbacks, they may feel as though they've been transported back into the traumatic event. This is called reexperiencing, and it often comes from out of the blue and causes extreme distress.

* **Trying to avoid reminders of the trauma.** People with PTSD may push away bad memories and stuff their emotions. They may also stay away from places and people that remind them of the trauma.

* **Having troublesome thoughts about themselves.** They may blame themselves, become extremely depressed, and avoid others, believing they're dangerous for others to be around. Sometimes traumatized people have difficulty remembering the details of the trauma.

* **Feeling constantly on high alert.** People with PTSD often feel jumpy and uneasy, as though something bad is about to happen. They may try to escape these feelings or the memories they bring up by abusing alcohol and drugs, or by engaging in risky activities or self-destructive behaviors.

All of these symptoms can cause people to have a great deal of trouble creating and maintaining relationships. They can also interfere with feeling happy and functioning at school or at work.

Note that only a trained mental health professional can diagnose a serious illness like PTSD. So if you feel you may have PTSD, please talk to a trusted adult so you can get appropriate help. And don't worry: there are lots of effective treatments for PTSD.

Concluding Thoughts

The death of a brother or sister doesn't always result in depression, poor adjustment, or PTSD. As mentioned, there numerous ways to respond to losing a sibling. Some teens report that they are able to adjust after losing a sibling, and some even report a great deal of growth. When families are close and maintain open communication, this seems to help teens more easily understand the meaning of their loss. In some families, there's a great deal of support for surviving siblings, helping them feel safe and trusting of their parents. And sometimes teens use the experience of losing a sibling to death to explore religion and create more spirituality in their lives.

In part 2 of this book, you'll become more familiar with the variety of ways teens cope after losing a brother or sister. This will probably help you better understand how you're coping. It may also help you feel less alone in your grief.

Coping Styles

chapter 4

Understanding Coping Styles

Just as no two individuals grieve the same way, no two individuals cope the same way. Here, in part 2 of the book, I'll help you get to know your own coping style. Dealing with the death of a brother or sister is a unique experience, and the specific relationship you had with your sibling doesn't apply to anybody else in this world. In addition, how you cope will be affected by others around you who are also grieving, who are trying to help you, or who don't know what to say. For all of these reasons, and more, your loss is your own; it belongs to you.

Sometimes grieving teens feel ignored or brushed aside, or as though how they're coping with the death of their sibling is less important than how their parents are coping. I hope that this part of the book provides you with a language to describe how you're coping, along with the feeling that you aren't alone as you work through your grief.

The general coping styles you'll read about in this part of the book come from careful research on my part, exploring the few studies of grieving teens that are available, and also from my experience as a professor and therapist. But because research in this area is currently so limited, there are probably other over-all styles, beyond the ones I've covered. Also, be aware that the styles I cover are generalizations. Most teens don't fit entirely into one style, and most don't have all the attributes of a certain style. These are just broad but useful outlines.

Your Style of Coping

The main element in this chapter is a quiz you can take to see if you might be coping primarily in one of the ways covered in chapters 5 through 8. Alternatively, you might find that you can relate to every style of coping and the examples in every chapter. That's not a bad thing. Because every relationship, life, and death is unique, it's normal and even healthy to feel different about yourself, your sibling, and your family at different times.

It's also important to know that you don't need to label yourself. As mentioned, the coping styles I describe are more like summaries or generalizations. Your own experience doesn't have to match any of them, and it's perfectly okay if it doesn't. Remember, you are the best expert on you. There's no need to force yourself into any particular category if it's not helpful. Trust yourself. Most of all, understand that your grief experience matters and should be honored.

As you'll read in this part of the book, sometimes teens turn to unhealthy choices like drinking or taking drugs to deal with their emotions. While there are better choices to make, if you've done this you aren't a bad person, and you aren't doomed. However, as you begin to understand your experience more deeply, my hope is that one day soon you'll be able to cope in healthier ways.

Here's a list of factors that might help you cope in a healthy way, followed by a list of factors that might stand in the way of healthy coping. Keep in mind that these lists are just suggestions to get you thinking about your own experience. As you read through the lists, you might want to keep your journal or the worksheet available at the website for this book close to hand, to write down some of your own ideas about things that might help or hurt as you cope with your grief.

What May Help

* Having caring and supportive people around you, including extended family members who can help with problem solving during hard times

* Having an easygoing personality and a history of coping with difficult situations by using positive strategies like art, breathing exercises, athletics, or talking to others

* Living in an area with lots of community resources, like good schools, job opportunities and training, community colleges, and military options

* Not having experienced many traumatic events in the past

* Having had some physical distance from the death when it happened and hearing fewer details about it

* The death not being very recent

What May Hurt

* Having parents or extended family members who aren't talking about the loss, who have shut themselves off from others, or who you've never felt particularly close with

* Having a history of mental health challenges, feeling very emotional, or feeling like you become numb or disconnected when bad things happen

* Lacking stable housing or living in poverty, feeling unsafe, or living in an area that has high crime rates or few or no community resources or opportunities for jobs or education

* Having been exposed to many traumatic events in the past

* Witnessing the death or hearing about many of the details, especially if the death was violent or painful

* The death being very recent

Preparing to Take the Quiz

When you complete the following quiz, take your time. Consider the multiple-choice answers, and then identify which one you relate to *most* of the time. You might want to write your answer to each in your journal. If you take the quiz at different times, you may find that your answers change, perhaps depending on how long it's been since your sibling died. So you might want to take it again someday for new insight into how you're coping. Before you begin, here are a few pointers on the quiz:

* **You may identify with all of the coping styles.** Your feelings and ways of coping may vary depending on how you're doing on a given day or how much time has passed since your sibling died.

* **Keep your journal at hand.** As you do the quiz, take some time to write about any thoughts or emotions that come up. This may help you claim ownership of what you're reading and feeling. It will also allow you to become an expert in your own coping style. Later, when you're ready, you can use this information to help others understand your coping style and how they can help you. (We'll talk about that more in part 3 of the book.)

* **Be prepared to experience many different emotions.** Some of the items in the quiz may bring up strong feelings. If you find yourself too upset, just skip that question or even skip the quiz altogether for now and then come back when you're ready.

Exercise: Identifying Your Coping Style

My friends are going out to a movie, and they've asked me to come along. I don't drive and could use a ride from my parents.

A. I don't want to bother my mom or dad because they've got more important things to worry about. I might get a ride from someone else or just stay home, but I won't burden my parents.

B. I ask myself, *What would my sibling do if he or she were here?* Then I do that.

C. I forget about going out with my friends—and maybe feel angry about it because I don't really relate to them anymore anyway.

D. I might ask my mom or dad for a ride when it seems like a good time. But it's so hard to tell when that might be that I may just ask someone else for a ride.

In the weeks following my sibling's death,

A. I saw how sad my parents were and tried really hard not to get in the way or make things worse. I tried to help them out by making phone calls, answering the door when visitors arrived, and doing well in school so that they wouldn't have to be distracted by me.

B. I tried to make my parents feel better by doing what my brother or sister would have done. I talked about my sibling a lot so people wouldn't forget about him or her.

C. I withdrew from everyone because no one could understand how I was feeling. Sometimes my emotions felt so strong, and then at other times I felt completely numb. I felt like people treated me differently, and I might have tried drinking or taking drugs to help me feel better.

D. I felt sad, lonely, and confused, but there were people to talk to about it. I had to get up the confidence to do that, though.

When I think about the future,

A. I wonder what will happen to me if I have to keep trying to take care of everybody else. I worry I won't ever be able to do what I want to do again.

B. I'll try to be sure nobody ever forgets my sibling, and I might even try to pick up where my brother or sister left off, such as by taking some of the same courses, getting involved in my sibling's favorite after-school activities, or getting closer to my sibling's friends.

C. I wonder if I'll be okay. I feel like I'm spiraling downward and there's nobody to catch me.

D. I'm not sure what's going to happen in my life, but I have some support, and I hope I'll get through life okay.

Since my sibling died, this is what I've worked on or struggled with the most:

A. How to help my family in practical and emotional ways, like funeral arrangements, pitching in around the house, and stepping up to handle tasks that my parents took care of before.

B. Trying to honor the memory of my sibling and finding ways to make sure people don't forget about him or her.

C. Not feeling connected to friends, family, and other signifi-cant people in my life, because nobody understands.

D. How to cope with my feelings and ask questions when everyone around me is grieving in different ways.

When I think about my brother or sister,

A. I keep feeling like my family will never get over the death because everyone seems so destroyed by it. It makes me want to do something to help move everyone forward.

B. I feel like I should have died instead. Not because I'm suicidal, but because it's so clear that my sibling left such a big hole to be filled that nothing I do can ever measure up.

C. I feel totally alone, overwhelmed, and even pissed off to the point of wanting to escape my current surroundings.

D. I feel many emotions: sad, confused, overwhelmed, angry... But I feel like eventually I might be able to find some peace with it. Depending on how I'm feeling on a given day, that seems more or less possible.

In regard to what I want to do with my life moving forward,

A. I might have to give up some of my plans to make sure my family will be okay.

B. I might need to pursue the goals and dreams my sibling had (for siblings old enough to have goals and dreams). Or I might think about the person my sibling would have become and try to follow that direction (especially with younger siblings). It's pretty clear that I need to become more like my brother or sister in some way.

C. I don't know what will happen to me or if I'll ever feel complete again. I picture myself as alone and confused, wandering aimlessly through life.

D. I hope I can stick to my original plans and stay true to myself while finding ways to honor my brother or sister. It might be tough.

Scoring

Count the number of As, Bs, Cs, and Ds in your responses. Whichever letter you have the most of is your main coping style.

Key

If you answered mostly As, you may identify most with the old soul (chapter 5).

If you answered mostly Bs, you may identify most with the replacement (chapter 6).

If you answered mostly Cs, you may identify most with the breakaway (chapter 7).

If you answered mostly Ds, you may identify most with the rubber band (chapter 8).

Once you've identified your coping style, you can jump right to that particular chapter if you want. I recommend reading that chapter a few times. Sometimes you'll notice important details on the second or even third reading. If you find that you don't have a clear score and instead have one or two of several different letters, you may want to start with the chapter 8, "The Rubber Band," which discusses a more balanced coping style. And however you answered, I recommend that you read all of the chapters in part 2 eventually. You may find information that's helpful to you or examples that resonate with your own experience in any of them. As you learn more about each coping style, you'll gain a greater understanding of your own ways of coping.

Concluding Thoughts

One important note: As with the quiz above, reading the stories of the teens in chapters 5 through 8 may bring up strong emotions. As you read on, be patient and gentle with yourself and give yourself permission to close the book and walk away when you need to. Just be sure to come back when you're ready.

chapter 5

The Old Soul

Sometimes I'm so busy taking care of everyone else that I wonder who's going to take care of me.

—Becca, age seventeen

Do you ever feel like Becca? Maybe after your brother or sister died, you stepped up to take on new tasks and roles, and now you sometimes worry about growing up too fast. And perhaps as you take care of others, you find that instead of feeling closer to them, you seem to be drifting further away. Maybe your family members are relying on you so much that they don't see how the extra work you're doing is taking a toll on you. If any of that sounds familiar, you may be an old soul in your coping style.

Teens who are old souls may feel pressure to help other family members cope with the loss, but in the long run they can end up feeling isolated or even resentful about having to grow up too quickly. People around teens who are old souls tend to view them as strong and independent and think they're coping better than expected. As a result, they may not realize that these teens could probably use some help in their own grieving. To see how this plays out, let's take a look at Becca's story.

✳ *Becca's Story*

Becca's brother, Joseph, committed suicide at home when he was fifteen and she was seventeen. Becca was at a friend's house when it happened. She and Joseph had been very close, but they were also very different: she liked hanging out with her friends, whereas Joseph stayed home more and spent a lot of time hanging out with their mom.

Becca had known Joseph was being bullied at school and she'd tried to help him. Her advice had been to ignore the bullies. She told Joseph, "The more of a reaction you give them, the more they'll pick on you. Just pretend it doesn't bother you."

Becca blamed herself for Joseph's suicide and wondered if she should have given him different advice. A lot of people told her that you can't stop someone from killing himself, but she thought that if she'd been home that night, she could have talked Joseph down or given him CPR if she'd found him in time. Instead, her mother was the one to find Joseph. Since then, Becca has noticed that her mom spends a lot of time in bed, sitting in Joseph's room, or just crying.

Becca decided that it was her job to take care of her mother, and she took on that role 100 percent. She knew it would have made Joseph proud to see her come home from school to make her mother lunch, and then cook dinner each night. One time her mom smiled at her and said, "Well, at least I have you, Becca. You don't let me down." Becca felt guilty. Before Joseph died, Becca had never felt this close to her mom. Now that Becca was taking such good care of her mom and they were getting along so well, she felt bad about taking attention away from Joseph. Sometimes she felt embarrassed and even sick to her stomach.

Meanwhile, Becca's dad started working late. So Becca also made sure to have dinner for him when he got home, and she sat with him while he ate. One night he said, "I was always glad you were social. You never would have done something like this." She felt confused and guilty again. She was glad that her dad appreciated what she was doing, but she felt like she was betraying Joseph.

Ultimately, Becca just felt stuck. With her dad gone most of the day and her mom seeming helpless, it seemed to Becca that she had to make sure the house was clean, answer the phone, and manage visits from well-wishers. Whenever people asked, she told them her family was doing fine.

At school, Becca's grades rose from Cs to As, and her guidance counselor told her that she could get into any community college she wanted. But Becca thought college would have to wait, because she needed to stay at home to make sure her mom and dad were okay. Becca felt like she couldn't talk to anyone about how she was feeling because everyone kept saying how well she was doing, and she didn't want to let anyone down.

Sometimes at night, after Becca turned out the lights and was by herself in bed, she had trouble sleeping. The house seemed so quiet with Joseph gone. She'd lie there wishing for her old life back: Joseph complaining about bullies; her best friend, Lisa, doing her makeup; herself making plans to get the boy she liked, Will, to talk to her; and just feeling normal. Yet Becca worried that if she went back to being her old self again—or if she were to cry or wonder why Joseph had to kill himself and change everything—her whole world would fall apart.

Can You Relate to Becca?

Let's take a look at a few specific aspects of Becca's experience that you may relate to.

Becca didn't feel like a carefree teen anymore. Before Joseph died, life had been a lot more normal and Becca had mostly done things that made her happy: hanging out with friends, talking about boys, and being involved in after-school activities. Her mom and dad took care of the family, and Becca felt like she was just a kid. Sometimes that had bugged her, and she'd even wished her parents would treat her like a grown-up. But when Joseph died, Becca's parents had a tough time coping, and Becca felt like she had to take care of everyone, even though it meant growing up too soon.

Ask yourself: Have you ever felt like you should take care of your parents because they're so upset over the death of your sibling? Do you maybe also have younger siblings that you're more in charge of now because it seems harder for your mom or dad to care for them?

Becca looked like she was doing fine on the outside, but she was hurting on the inside. Becca didn't want her parents to have to worry about her, so she tried to take care of herself and do better in school. Her grades improved and she acted more mature. But when she was alone, she felt sad, hurt, and confused. She wondered why everything had to change and wished things could go back to how they had been.

Ask yourself: When you're alone, is that the only time you let yourself think about and feel your own feelings? Is that because you want to protect your family? Do you spend most of your time trying to be there for them?

Becca used to love being with her friends, but now she stays home more. It's normal and healthy for teens to want to spend time with friends, away from their family. That's part of how you learn about who you are and who you want to be: by spending time with people other than your family members. Plus, sometimes spending time with other people makes you appreciate who you are. But Becca stopped doing that because she felt her family needed her. Joseph had stayed home a lot, and Becca felt she should take his place.

Ask yourself: Do you ever wish for your old life back, doing things like spending time with friends and just having fun? Do you feel as though your sibling left a confusing mess for your whole family that you need to clean up?

Things You Might Be Thinking

If you're an old soul, you may have some of the common thoughts listed below. For each, I've provided an example from a teen to make it more concrete.

* *I'm hurting but nobody notices.*

   Lainey, age sixteen: "People keep telling me how great it is that I'm being so helpful to my mom because she's so torn up over my brother's death. They seem to think I'm doing fine, maybe better than fine, but the fact is, I cry and feel sick to my stomach, and nobody is there for me the way I'm there for my mom."

✱ *I don't understand why this had to happen.*

Bryan, age fourteen: "I don't get why my baby sister had to die. She was so young and helpless. I'm still here, and I got to live for fourteen years. It feels like my mom and dad are angry that my sister didn't get to live a longer life. But none of it is my fault, so why do I feel so guilty?"

✱ *If something happens to me, my parents will never recover. They're barely hanging on now.*

Rita, eighteen: "I'm the parent now that my brother has died, kind of. I do the dishes and the laundry. I handle phone calls. I make sure my little sisters are ready for school and that they have lunch packed. Sometimes I get really anxious thinking about what would happen if I died too. Who would take care of my little sisters?"

✱ *I'm not enough.*

Murray, fifteen: "I try so hard to be good. I try to show my grandparents and parents that I'm in control and doing great in school so they don't have to worry. But they don't even seem to care. I'm never good enough."

✳ *It's so unfair.*

Leilani, thirteen: "This sucks. I'm there for everybody, but nobody's there for me. How is that fair?"

✳ *I can't let anybody see how I really feel, because everyone is already so upset.*

Augusten, nineteen: "It's better for me to stuff my feelings because they're not pretty. If people knew what was going on in my head, they wouldn't be complimenting me so much. They'd be more upset. So I keep it to myself and focus on helping others."

Things You Might Be Doing

Certain behaviors are more common among teens who are old souls. Read through the behaviors below and the example for each. Are you doing any of these things?

✳ Spending more time with adults and less time with friends

Lainey has been putting in more hours with her grandparents now that her mother is grieving the loss of Lainey's brother. Her grandparents live across the street and need lots of help—help Lainey's mother used to provide. Lainey also spends more time talking to her family's pastor, her mother's friends, and teachers at school, updating everyone on her family's situation and acting as a go-between for her mother.

✳ Helping make funeral arrangements

Rita helped choose a casket for her brother and clothes for him to wear. She coordinated the meals that well-wishers brought to the house and picked out music for the ceremony. While she was proud to take on some of the responsibility, she also felt overwhelmed by some of the tasks and thought her parents should have been more involved. It felt like a heavy responsibility to talk to the funeral director so much.

✳ Taking phone calls from well-wishers

Bryan's new job at home is being the "phone guy." His parents seem too overwhelmed and sad to answer, yet Bryan hates the sound of the phone constantly ringing, so he handles calls for the family. He even wrote out a standard speech to use when people ask how his parents are doing. He doesn't think about the job too much anymore; he just accepts that it's part of his life at home now.

✳ Studying hard for tests and focusing more on school or doing well in extracurricular activities

In the year following his brother's death, Murray decided to work harder in school and raise his grades. He thought this would be one less thing for his parents to worry about. And in a way, he enjoyed the challenge. Plus, it felt good to focus on school instead of life at home. He spent more time at the library and even got a leading role in the school play.

✻ Reassuring everyone you're fine, even though inside, you might not be

For Augusten, it feels easier, at least in the short run, to hide his true feelings around others instead of expressing himself. He also worries that his thoughts are abnormal because sometimes they're unkind, jealous, or critical of his dead brother. So he puts on a smiling face and tells others that he's coping well.

The Challenge of Being an Old Soul

Just like Becca and the teens whose examples appeared above, as an old soul you may feel caught between being you (a teen) and being a grown-up. Inside, you may wish that life had stayed the same so you could focus on yourself and your needs. On the outside, though, you may feel that your parents or others need you to take care of them or the situation. It might even seem that they expect you to do so. Sometimes you may find comfort in being in charge—and you may even be really good at it. But you don't really want to be the go-to person, and you may think you shouldn't have so many responsibilities, especially when you're grieving yourself. At the same time, you may not want to make life, as it is now, any harder for anybody else, or make it all about you and your feelings. You're stuck because you're stretched in two opposite directions: helping others and taking care of yourself. You may feel guilty when you focus on yourself, but you may also feel resentful about how much you're focusing on others.

Other Coping Styles You Might Relate To

Check out chapter 7, "The Breakaway." Sometimes when the pressure to grow up quickly becomes too intense, teens fall into unhealthy behaviors like drinking, doing drugs, or engaging in risky behaviors. You may relate to feeling or acting this way. Chapter 6, "The Replacement," might hit home for you too, because it covers another common reaction to feeling that you're under too much pressure: trying to be more like your brother or sister. You might feel that this is what your parents and others want.

What You Can Do About It

In part 3 of the book, you'll find many tools, tips, and exercises to help you on your journey toward healing:

* In chapter 10, "Don't Believe Everything You Think," you'll begin to explore how the way you think about yourself has changed due to your sibling's death, and how to bring some new perspective to the table by challenging those assumptions. Keep an eye out for exercises that focus on substituting healthier, more realistic thoughts for distorted thoughts.

* In chapter 11, "Telling Your Story," you'll find suggestions for how to express yourself and tell the story of your loss from *your* point of view. Your voice is an important one that needs to be heard, not because of the roles you've taken on in the aftermath of your sibling's death, but because of who you are—unique, wonderful,

and talented. You deserve a special space for talking about your loss in a format and style that works for you.

* In chapter 12, "Making Meaning," you'll learn some new ways to talk about life as it is now and also learn how to ask for help. You might appreciate the concrete suggestions for how to help others respect boundaries you create—boundaries that allow you to be a regular teenager, rather than being stuck in all of the responsibilities you've taken on.

Concluding Thoughts

Take a deep breath. Some of the information in this chapter might have been hard to read. It may have brought up some sad, scary, or anxious feelings. Learning about your coping style is likely to help you feel better in the long run, but in the short term, it may be hard to face the fact that you perhaps haven't allowed yourself to really feel your grief in a strong way. You may also be a bit resentful that others seem to expect you to take care of them without thinking about how they might take care of you. Then you might feel guilty for being resentful. The first step in feeling better is to *let yourself feel*. So how do you feel about being an old soul?

You may find it helpful to fill out the "Coping Styles" worksheet available online to help you think through what you've read, or grab your journal and take some time to write down your thoughts and feelings after reading this chapter. What you write doesn't even have to make sense, but it can be helpful to have an outlet for jotting down whatever comes to mind as you process what you've just read in this chapter

————————— chapter 6 —————————

The Replacement

I can't help but think the wrong child died. There's only one
way to make this right, and that's to become more like my
brother.

—Eric, age sixteen

Do you ever feel like Eric? Perhaps after your brother or sister died you began to feel as though your family, and maybe
your friends, teachers, and other important people in your
life, thought the wrong child had died. This is a heavy feeling to struggle with. Eric is coping with it by trying to become
more like his brother because he believes that will help others
cope with their grief, and that it will also ease the guilt he feels
because he wasn't the one who died.

It's difficult to be surrounded by so much pain and loss after
a sibling dies, and sometimes teens get the idea they don't matter as much as their sibling did. Like Becca, Eric feels the need
to step up and do something to help his family with their grief,
and his solution is to become more like his brother. I call this
coping style "the replacement" because it involves trying to
fill a sibling's shoes. However, as teens with this coping style
become more and more like their sibling, they eventually find

that they no longer recognize themselves, or they start feeling as though they don't have their own, unique identity. Yet being a teen is all about finding out who you are, so becoming more like a brother or sister can cause teens to feel very lost. Sometimes teens adopt this coping style because their parents or others encourage them to take on their sibling's hobbies and habits. This can be comforting to parents and other family members, so they may not realize that these teens need to have permission to stay true to themselves. To see how this plays out, let's take a closer look at Eric's story.

✳ Eric's Story

Eric's older brother, Luke, was eighteen when he died after a one-year struggle with a rare form of brain cancer. Eric was only twenty months younger than Luke, and they had enjoyed the same activities, especially basketball and baseball. Eric often felt that because he was a little younger, he was trying to measure up to his brother in all aspects of life. For example, they used to fight, in a friendly way, over who would get to date a certain girl, who teachers liked best, and who was more popular.

Of course, Luke treated Eric like a kid brother—because he was. He coached him in sports and always pushed him to be better. One of his favorite lines was "You can't catch up with me, bro!" Eric usually felt like he was living in Luke's shadow, given how Luke was just a little more coordinated, hit more home runs, and smiled a little easier when making new friends.

As Luke's cancer progressed, his vision and balance became compromised, so he developed new interests to replace sports, including painting. He excelled in this new hobby, even with the limitations his cancer caused. The high school had an exhibition of Luke's paintings, and it was written up in the local paper. After a follow-up story describing Luke's fight with cancer, Luke received numerous donations of art supplies. Adult cancer survivors started visiting him, and the school basketball team hosted a paint-a-thon to raise money for cancer research. Luke also set up an online journal focused on his battle with cancer, and soon he had hundreds of followers. When Luke was in the hospital or was feeling too weak, Eric tried to update the journal. But he couldn't focus and felt at a loss, so eventually their mother took over.

When Luke died, he was commemorated at the school. A couple of pictures of him playing sports were hung in the gym, and several of his paintings were displayed in the school library. The family lived in a somewhat small town, and the mayor even made a speech about Luke's dedication to athletics, art, and poetry. After the speech, he told Eric to keep Luke's legacy alive. He also presented the school with a check for a new "Luke's Legacy" scholarship, to be awarded to the student showing the most dedication to athletics and art, in addition to academics.

Throughout this time, Eric increasingly felt that what made him unique wasn't important. Basically, he felt as though the wrong child had died. In Eric's mind, Luke's successes seemed to highlight the fact that Eric could never measure up. It seemed to Eric that the only solution was to fulfill Luke's legacy as best he could. He began devoting his time after school to painting with the supplies Luke had left behind. He began updating Luke's online journal in Luke's own voice, as if Luke were talking from heaven, and he volunteered to organize the basketball team's paint-a-thon the following year. He also started wearing the "Team Luke" clothes that Luke had worn to the hospital for chemo. Toward the end of his junior year, he dated Luke's former girlfriend, Tara. He also won the "Luke's Legacy" scholarship that year. At the award ceremony, someone asked how he felt about winning, and he said, "Luke was an all-around hero. He was the best brother, and now I'm making sure I don't mess up all the great things he did. I wouldn't be who I am if he hadn't shown me who I was supposed to be, which is Luke's brother. I hope when people see me, they see Luke and remember he's still here with us, maybe even more than before."

Meanwhile, inside, Eric dreamed of having his own life and not trying to be so much like Luke. He was keeping his brother alive so everyone could be as happy as possible, but he was starting to hate himself. He wondered why everyone had loved Luke so much and why he himself had always been second best. On the second anniversary of Luke's death, Eric used black paint to paint over his face in a bunch of family pictures. Then he walked to the highway and hitched a ride. A truck driver picked him up, but by the time they got to the next town, Eric realized that he didn't want to run away from home, and that it wasn't the answer to escaping Luke's powerful influence. So Eric headed back home, even though he felt more lost than ever.

Can You Relate to Eric?

Let's take a look at a few specific aspects of Eric's experience that you may relate to.

Losing Luke made Eric feel confused about his identity. For his entire life, Eric had used knowing who Luke was to understand who he was. We all learn about ourselves by comparing ourselves to our siblings. When Luke died, Eric couldn't seem to identify his own hobbies or interests. Instead of learning about himself, he gravitated more and more toward what Luke had done and been interested in—what made him Luke.

Ask yourself: After your brother or sister died, did you feel a sense of emptiness or confusion about your own personality or self-understanding? Did you ask yourself, *Who am I, now that my sibling has died? Am I the same person or somebody different? Do I need to be more like my brother or sister, or less?* If you asked yourself these questions, did you have trouble answering them?

Eric felt pressured to be more like his brother. As Luke fought cancer, he became a hero in the community and won the support and admiration of many people. Eric, who had always felt like he couldn't quite measure up anyway, was encouraged to continue "Luke's legacy," including by the mayor. For many people, Luke had been a symbol of hope and courage, and Eric took this to mean that he should continue in Luke's footsteps. So he wore Luke's clothes, continued Luke's online journal, and kept the paint-a-thon going. While all of this looked good on the outside and may have fulfilled others' expectations, becoming more and more like Luke made Eric feel emptier inside.

Ask yourself: Have you tried to adopt any of your sibling's qualities, hobbies, or friendships since he or she died? Have you done so because you feel this is what your family and friends want, because it seems like the right thing to do, or because becoming more like your brother or sister may help you fill the gap in your life? Is it satisfying for you to try to fill your siblings shoes, or do you feel as though you're selling yourself short?

Eric felt guilty that his brother died, not him. Though he may not have been aware of it, Eric concluded that his family, friends, and community felt the wrong sibling had died. The ways they celebrated Luke's life and mourned his death left Eric feeling guilty, as though even after Luke's death he was still competing with his brother—and still didn't measure up. Ultimately, he even tried running away from home because he hadn't figured out how not to feel so isolated and hurt in that environment.

Ask yourself: Do the ways your family members, friends, and other people in your life talk about your sibling and grieve make you feel excluded or as though the wrong child died? Does this give rise to a sense of frustration, resentment, or guilt? Do you wonder if anybody would miss you in the same way if you died? And do you ever feel like escaping from the environments that make you feel you have to fill your sibling's shoes?

Things You Might Be Thinking

If you're trying to replace your sibling and fill his or her shoes, you may have some of the common thoughts listed below. For each, I've provided an example to make it more concrete:

* *I don't know who I am anymore.*

   Latasha, age fourteen: "I just started high school, and everybody is figuring out what clothes they want to wear, what music they want to listen to, and who they want to hang out with. I don't know if I should try harder to hang out with my brother's friends who are in elementary school, or if I should try to make new friends. I feel like people expect me to stay friends with his friends, but I really don't know what I want."

* *People don't want me; they want my sibling.*

    Maude, age eighteen: "It's pretty clear that people miss my sister more than they would miss me if I died. To make them happy, I'm selling myself short and turning into the person they want to see. The happier it makes them, the sadder it makes me, because who I am doesn't seem to matter as much as who my sister was."

* *I need to fill the roles my sibling once filled.*

    Moses, age thirteen: "My brother was the peacemaker in the family. He was the person you went to when you were in a fight because he was a really good listener. Now I'm the peacemaker, so when my parents fight, they come to me."

* *I need to be somebody else.*

    Alyssabeth, age fifteen: "My parents were trying for another boy after they lost my brother, but I came along instead. I try to do boy things, like play sports, and be athletic, because that's who they want me to be."

* *I'm worthless.*

    Bennett, age seventeen: "Nobody cares about me the way they loved my brother. He was a really good student, an all-around nice kid, and popular. He had everything. Then they look at me... I'm pretty average, I guess, when I compare myself to him, and that makes me feel like I'm no good. Like, if he was so great and he died, how can I live up to the person he was when I'm not good enough?"

Things You Might Be Doing

Certain behaviors are more common among replacement teens. Read through the behaviors below and the example for each. Are you doing any of these things?

* Spending more time on hobbies or interests your sibling enjoyed

  Alyssabeth's brother was an athlete, and her mother still displays some of his Little League sports trophies on their mantle. Alyssabeth has never enjoyed team sports and likes them even less because she's felt awkward and uncoordinated since becoming a teenager. Still, she knows her mom would be disappointed if she didn't play on at least one team, so she's decided not to audition for the school play this year in order to make time for playing soccer.

* Avoiding thinking about your own future or changing your future plans

  Maude should be focusing on going to college next year, but she's avoiding it because her sister didn't get the chance to go. She feels that she isn't entitled to a future because her sister was robbed of one. Although she'd like to go to business school, Maude's decided that if she does go to college, she'll probably study nursing because her sister wanted to be a nurse. Maude thinks that if she becomes a nurse, it might help her parents feel as though her sister's death wasn't completely in vain.

✳ Thinking of ways to escape

Bennett feels as though he's worthless when compared with his brother. He also feels that the longer he stays in his hometown, the more people will associate him with his brother and feel disappointed because he isn't his brother. To escape the constant feeling of judgment, he's considered going to military school or applying for a school exchange program so he can move someplace where nobody knows him.

The Challenge of Being a Replacement

Just like Eric and the teens in the examples above, as a replacement you may feel that you can no longer live your own life and move forward on the journey to becoming you. You may feel pressured to become more like your sibling. While the important people in your life may compliment you for doing that, you could feel conflicted because trying to live up to others' expectations prevents you from expressing your true feelings or exploring who you are. You might feel as though you're missing fun or exciting opportunities or social situations you'd enjoy simply because your sibling might have chosen a differ-. ent path. At the same time, you're trying to ease others' grief by carrying on your sibling's legacy, and you may feel proud of yourself for helping your family, friends, and others cope with their grief. You may even enjoy taking over some of your sibling's roles and responsibilities. However, you could also feel resentful or wonder if you're missing out on other experiences in life. You can't know if you're on the right path to becoming who you want to be if you don't step outside of your sibling's identity to explore what it means to be yourself.

Other Coping Styles You Might Relate To

If you haven't already read it, check out chapter 5, "The Old Soul." Teens who are old souls also feel pressured to take care of others who are grieving; but they do so not by becoming more like their sibling, but by taking on more responsibility than a teen should have to. You might relate to that coping style since you've taken on the replacement style in an effort to ease the pain of others. In addition, you may find it helpful to read chapter 7, "The Breakaway," because sometimes teens who feel pressured to take on their sibling's identity end up seeking escape in risky activities, including drinking or doing drugs. Perhaps you've tried to cope in this way too. Finally, take a look at chapter 8, "The Rubber Band," where you'll learn that it isn't always unhealthy to want to take on some of your sibling's qualities. You may actually discover new aspects of yourself and your identity by trying to follow in your sibling's footsteps, and this could help you cope in a healthy way. Rubber band teens are able to integrate the loss of a sibling into their life story in a way that doesn't feel as though they're losing themselves.

What You Can Do About It

In part 3 of the book, you'll find many tools, tips, and exercises to help you on your journey toward healing:

* In chapter 10, "Don't Believe Everything You Think," you'll explore your thought processes and learn that while you may mean well, your thoughts and feelings about your sibling's death may be influencing how you react to others' expectations. In that chapter, keep an eye out for techniques that help empower you to respond to the important people in your life who seem to be expecting you to fill your sibling's shoes.

* In chapter 11, "Telling Your Story," you'll learn how to express your understanding of your story of loss and grief in a way that will help reestablish a sense of who you are, recounting your loss and experiences from your own point of view.

* In chapter 12, "Making Meaning," you'll find suggestions about how you can live your own life—as yourself—with meaning and purpose, while also honoring your sibling. It will help you explore how your sibling's death has affected your sense of your identity and support you in separating yourself from expectations, whether from others or yourself.

Concluding Thoughts

Sometimes information that helps you learn about yourself can be comforting. It can be enormously healing to discover that you aren't alone, including in how you cope, and that others have responded in similar ways to a sibling's death. On the other hand, it can be shocking to read stories about teens who, like you, tried to fill their sibling's shoes, and to relate so much to those stories. Whether you're feeling jolted or uplifted by what you've just read, it's worth taking some time to reflect upon what the replacement coping style means for you—in your life, and in your process with grief.

Consider taking some time to write about this in your journal, focusing on your thoughts and feelings, or using the "Coping Styles" worksheet available at http://www.newharbinger.com/32493. What you write doesn't need to make sense. It's often helpful to just have an outlet for your thoughts and feelings, including those that arise as you process what you read in this chapter.

chapter 7

The Breakaway

What's wrong with me? I feel so alone. Everybody treats me differently than before, like I'm broken. It makes me want to hide from the world, lash out, and do something crazy all at the same time.

—Tommy, age fifteen

Do you ever feel like Tommy? Like the teens in the two previous chapters (old soul and replacement teens), Tommy is also responding to the behavior of people around him, but his response has been to turn his grief inward and focus more on his own thoughts and feelings. While some teens might seek a closer relationship with family members after a sibling dies, others, Tommy included, feel as though they don't belong anywhere and literally break away from the people who care about them. In some ways, that's natural. As mentioned, being a teen means learning about who you are as an individual, and that involves moving away from your family and toward friends who are more like you. But sometimes when teens lose a sibling, their friends may think they're different and no longer easy to relate to. Has this happened to you?

If you can identify with being a breakaway teen, you might feel that you'd like your friends to support you more and ask how you're doing in the aftermath of your loss. But at the same time, you may not want to be seen as different from others in your group while also feeling that your friends have already decided that you're different. This can make you feel very alone. You might even feel as though you've become unpopular simply because you have a sibling who died.

Breakaway teens may start avoiding their friends and family while trying to figure out what's wrong with them and how they can fit in again. And like most teens, they often crave excitement or seek out new experiences to help them figure out who they are. But without close connections to friends and family members, they might find themselves experimenting on their own with dangerous activities, including binge drinking, doing drugs, getting into fights, or stealing. They might feel that getting edgy will help them fit in again. If you've tried coping in this way, please know that you aren't alone—and that there are healthier options. To get a better idea of how this coping style plays out, let's take a look at Tommy's story.

✱ Tommy's Story

Tommy was fifteen when his sister, Isla, age seven, was killed by a drunk driver in broad daylight while crossing the street. Tommy came upon the scene while he was walking home from school and was stunned. Afterward he had nightmares and flashbacks of Isla being taken away in the ambulance. He was out of school for a few days for the funeral, but after that he felt ready to go back, see his friends, and try to get back to normal life, especially because life at home felt so sad, quiet, and different. But when he went back to school, all of his friends seemed awkward and nervous around him. He knew it was because Isla had died, but he didn't want to say anything about her death for fear it would make his friends act even stranger.

One day one of Tommy's teachers kept him after class to talk about his sister, and it made him feel even more out of place. He saw two friends leaving for lunch, and he felt angry because it seemed like he was being singled out. When he finally went outside, Jim and Nick, his two best friends, were laughing about something. Tommy said, "Hey guys, what's so funny?" But Nick wouldn't look him in the eye, and Jim just said, "Never mind. It's no big deal." Tommy felt embarrassed.

Tommy started to feel like his friends didn't want him around. He knew he was different now and that Isla's death was the reason, and he hated being singled out. He kept having nightmares and was feeling overwhelmed, so he started to look for ways to try to feel better. He started smoking weed with Jim after school, and he liked how it made him feel like his problems didn't belong to him anymore but to someone else. He also started making fun of the teacher who had kept him back after class that one day. He loved making the other kids laugh, even though he knew they mostly just felt sorry for him. Still, he felt like it made him look cool, as though he didn't care.

Tommy's parents were caught up in their own grief. They didn't answer the phone when the principal called to warn them about Tommy's frequent visits to her office, and they didn't seem to notice the smell of weed on his clothes. To Tommy, it felt as though they were absent, and he didn't know who to turn to for help. In addition, he wasn't even sure how to ask for help *or whether he really needed it. It was hard to figure out on his own, and it seemed like he didn't have anybody to talk to about his feelings.*

No matter what he did to try to get back to normal with his friends, Tommy still felt different. He started riding his bike back and forth across traffic, inviting his friends to watch him beat cars at the last minute. The whole time, he was thinking that he was cheating death in a way that Isla had not. He also looked for cars similar to the one that had killed Isla and threw rocks at them as they drove past. One time he and Jim broke the back windshield of a car, and it ended up in a fender bender. They were arrested and spent that night in jail, and then Tommy was on probation and Jim was sent to military school.

After that incident, Tommy's mom became more aware of his struggles and started taking him to psychiatrists, counselors, and group therapy. She got him a job, but he didn't show up to work. Meanwhile, he felt like no one could understand what it was like to be numb but feel too many feelings—to be hateful and angry and also to feel empty, all at the same time, and all the time. Even though he tried to fit in, he felt completely alone, and he thought no one could understand.

Can You Relate to Tommy?

Let's take a look at a few specific aspects of Tommy's experience that you may relate to.

Tommy had a hard time feeling connected to his friends.
After Isla's funeral, Tommy was looking forward to going back

to school, but when he did, he felt like he was being treated differently. His teacher keeping him after class made him feel as though he stood out even more. Tommy's efforts to reconnect with his friends, whether by trying to get involved in conversations, being the class clown, or taking part in risky activities, only seemed to isolate him further. Tommy felt like others just weren't able to treat him like the person he was before Isla died.

Ask yourself: Do you have trouble relating to your friends, teachers, or family members in the wake of your sibling's death? Do you feel as though others are making assumptions about your personality and believe that you've somehow become a different person, even though you don't feel like you've changed? Do your attempts to connect with others often make you feel even more alone?

Tommy's self-esteem was low, he was always angry, and he was having nightmares. After witnessing the scene of his sister's death, Tommy experienced painful reminders of what happened in the form of nightmares. He also felt angry, frustrated, and as though nobody understood him. This caused him to act out more in class and try to stand out in other ways so that people wouldn't define him by Isla's death. Unfortunately, he still felt like he was different. And as Tommy felt increasingly worse, his self-esteem sank even further, and he became increasingly angry more of the time. It was a vicious cycle.

Ask yourself: Are there any painful reminders of your sibling's death that keep popping up in your waking or dreaming life? These could be memories of the death itself, your parents' reactions, details you heard from others, or feelings that were overwhelming. Are you having nightmares or feeling anxious? Do these reminders make you feel abnormal, as though you're coping in a way that's completely different from how others around you respond to major losses?

Tommy didn't know who to turn to for help and sought relief in unhealthy activities. Because of his painful memories and feelings of isolation, Tommy turned to drugs and risky activities. He wanted to fit in with his friends, and he also wanted to stand out in ways other than being the kid whose sister died, but he chose extreme methods of doing so. Yet Tommy couldn't numb his sadness and loneliness completely, and he kept feeling as though his friends were judging him and making the situation worse. He wanted to be a "normal" teen, but because he wasn't getting much positive support from friends and family members, he didn't recognize that he was going too far and could seriously hurt himself. Then, by getting involved in risky activities, Tommy distanced himself further and further from the people who cared about him.

Ask yourself: Have you tried to numb yourself with drugs or alcohol, or maybe by the adrenaline high of getting involved in risky activities, like Tommy did? Did you hope that standing out in this way might cause your friends to see you differently and not just as somebody whose brother or sister died? Did these attempts work, or did you end up feeling more alone than before?

Things You Might Be Thinking

If you're a breakaway teen, you may have some of the common thoughts listed below. For each, I've provided an example to make it more concrete:

* *Am I supposed to move on already?*

  Janice, age sixteen: "I was hanging out with a friend, and I was just thinking and being quiet. My friend asked, 'What's wrong?' I thought, *My brother just died two weeks ago and you're asking me what's wrong?*"

* *I hurt inside.*

  Carmac, age thirteen: "I don't want to stand out and be different, but I feel like everyone can see how much I hurt. I cry a lot, and boys aren't supposed to cry. We're supposed to be tough, but I hurt so bad and just don't know what to do. It feels like somebody punched me in the stomach."

* *I don't belong.*

  Harald, age fourteen: "My friends think I'm weird. My teachers feel sorry for me. My mom and dad don't want to talk about my sister, and they don't ask me about school. I'm not the different one—everybody else is. I just feel like I don't fit in anywhere anymore."

* *The only way to feel better is to get rid of the pain.*

  Wyatt, age sixteen: "The only way to escape is to sleep, get high, or play video games all night long. When I'm just on my own and not doing anything, I can't stop thinking about everything that happened and how bad I feel. Sometimes I feel sick and sometimes I feel guilty, and if I'm not in a different head state, it's too much for me to deal with. Plenty of kids my age drink and do drugs anyway, I just do them by myself or a little more than others because it helps me forget."

* *I want everything to go back to normal.*

  Norma, age seventeen: "I hate the way this feels, and I wish my brother hadn't died. My life was good. I had a boyfriend, and I was having a good time at school. Then he died, which threw a grenade into everything and exploded my life. I want it to go back to normal."

* *I don't know who I am anymore.*

  Ginny, age eighteen: "I don't recognize myself. The happy, creative girl is gone. I don't think I'll ever feel happy again. My friends feel like aliens to me. I was getting along great with my stepfather and now he's like a brick wall—no emotion and so cold. What's wrong with me? Why can't I just get over it and move forward? Who am I turning into?"

Things You Might Be Doing

Certain behaviors are more common among breakaway teens. Read through the behaviors below and the example for each. Are you doing any of these things?

* Spending more time alone

  Carmac is finding it harder to be around other people because he's in deep emotional pain. He's embarrassed because he feels that, as a boy, he should be tougher. So he's withdrawn from his friends and family and is spending more time by himself. When he's alone, Carmac cries, tells himself he's a loser, and feels hopeless.

* Acting out in school or with parents

  Harald feels singled out by the adults and friends in his life. This frustrates him and makes him want to provoke people because he feels this is what they're doing to him. He's started playing music very loudly when his parents are trying to sleep, going out at night and turning over neighbors' trash cans, and walking out of classes and slamming the door while teachers are giving lessons.

* Drinking, doing drugs, or getting involved in other unhealthy activities

  Wyatt is exploring ways to push away his emotional pain and feelings of being different. Wyatt steals his dad's vodka and his mom's prescription pills and uses them when he's alone at night. He goes online to play video games and insults his fellow players through his headset. He also specifically seeks out the most brutal ways to kill other players' characters. When he's hanging out at friends' houses, Wyatt is always first to suggest raiding their parents' liquor cabinets, in part because he thinks this will help him fit in better. Recently, he's also started binge eating junk food to fill the emptiness he feels inside.

* Wishing you were somebody else

Ginny has been daydreaming about what life would be like if she'd been born into a different family. She feels guilty about this, but she's so unhappy that she fantasizes about being somebody completely different.

* Trying to control others or your own life, down to the tiniest details

Norma wants her old life back. She liked who she was and how things were going. But now everything feels so out of control, and she feels like everybody is watching her and judging her. In an effort to feel like she has some control or is in charge of something in her life, she's started restricting the food she eats and counting calories. Focusing on her outward appearance also provides a distraction from her breakup with her first serious boyfriend and the fact that she's failed every test at school since her brother died.

The Challenge of Being a Breakaway Teen

You may feel that the death of your sibling has made your friends, family members, or other people in your life see you differently and treat you differently. You may feel changed by your loss in ways you don't completely understand while also feeling that those changes are obvious to others. For teens, standing out and being different is often a good and exciting thing and a way to explore your identity. But the feeling of difference due to the death of a sibling can feel forced upon you and make you feel alone and uncomfortable or even uncool or unpopular. In any case, the journey to find out who you are has been interrupted, and you may be feeling as though you'll never truly find yourself.

In addition, when your friends don't seem to be there to help you cope with your loss, you might avoid them, even though they may be the very people who could help you feel better. And although standing out and taking risks is a normal part of being a teen, if you start drinking, doing drugs, or engaging in risky activities when you don't have social support, you may not notice whether you're going too far. That's the benefit of having friends to share experiences with or parents or other family members who are looking out for you. They help you draw a boundary between experimentation and behavior that goes too far. Without people beside you on this journey, you can end up very badly hurt. Yet even when you're in a group, if you try too hard to fit in and still go too far, your friends may not be sure how to help you or stop you. So you may be losing the perspective you need to realize when it's time put on the brakes.

Other Coping Styles You Might Relate To

If you haven't already, read both chapter 5, "The Old Soul," and chapter 6, "The Replacement," as you might relate to both of those coping styles. While teens with those styles are usually focused on making life easier for family members, friends, and others in the wake of their sibling's death, sometimes the pressure is too much and they feel the need to escape. They may do that by avoiding others or taking part in risky activities, just like breakaway teens. If the examples in this chapter seemed a little extreme to you, check out chapter 8, "The Rubber Band." Rubber band teens sometimes engage in risky activities, depending on how they're feeling, the people around them, and the messages they get from others about grief. But overall, they're more social and less isolated than most breakaway teens.

What You Can Do About It

In part 3 of the book, you'll find many tools, tips, and exercises to help you on your journey toward healing:

* Chapter 10, "Don't Believe Everything You Think," will help you explore some of the assumptions you may have that affect the choices you make, including choices that

may not be healthy for you. You'll learn a lot about the links between thoughts, feelings, and actions, along with some strategies for coping and healing.

* Chapter 11, "Telling Your Story," offers guidance on sharing the story of your loss from your own point of view. This will help you communicate your needs to others and let them know how you want them to connect with you. You don't have to be a supporting character in a story about your sibling's death and how it's affected your life—you can and should be the main character in your life. This will help you work with the feelings you're experiencing and ride the waves of grief in a safer way.

* If you feel like you're alone, angry, fighting to survive, and lashing out at the world, chapter 12, "Making Meaning," will help you shift to expressing the meaning of your feelings in ways that are healthier for you. In addition, chapter 12 will look at ways you can fit in with friends while also standing out as your own person—without resorting to drugs, alcohol, or dangerous activities.

Concluding Thoughts

I hope that reading this chapter has helped you feel less alone, as you now know that other teens are grieving the loss of their siblings and going through something similar to what you are.

You're in a difficult spot, and it's understandable that you might have turned to some less than healthy behaviors to try to feel better. Unfortunately, the choices you make now could end up hurting you badly in the short term or the long run, and ultimately, they will only make your pain worse. If you find yourself running away from your feelings by using substances, ask yourself, *What are my feelings, and why am I trying to stuff them? Is there a better way to communicate my pain? And might there be even one trusted adult in my life that I can talk to without feeling singled out or treated differently?* Although others may not always know how to discuss grief, you probably have caring people around you who want you to feel better. If you aren't ready to ask for help, I encourage you to turn to part 3 to learn more about how you can help yourself. But remember, although it may feel as though you're in this alone, you truly aren't. There is hope.

Finally, take some time to reflect on the thoughts and feelings that came up as you were reading this chapter. Then consider writing about whatever came up for you in your journal. What you write doesn't need to make sense. It's helpful to just have an outlet for your thoughts and feelings. You can also use the prompts on the "Coping Styles" worksheet available at the website for this book to work through your thoughts about what you've read.

chapter 8

The Rubber Band

When my brother first died, I missed him so much and I felt so alone. I didn't know how I would get through. Now that some time has passed and I've had some people to talk to, I'm learning how to live life without him. I still miss him, but I try to do things that would make him proud.

—Zarrah, age fourteen

Do you ever feel like Zarrah? Teens like Zarrah have many of the thoughts and feelings of old soul, replacement, and break-away teens (covered in chapters 5 through 7) and struggle with the death of their sibling in many different ways, especially immediately after the death. They grieve, cry, and sometimes feel helpless and confused. But as time passes they find ways to cope with grief that help them get through every day a bit more easily. Just like a rubber band, these teens feel stretched—maybe even to their limits on occasion—but with time they bounce back. This doesn't mean they aren't affected by their grief or that they don't experience symptoms. But they generally find ways to work with their grief and make it part of their daily life. For rubber band teens, surviving the loss of their sibling ultimately becomes part of their identity. For many teens, this is their primary coping style.

Rubber band teens like Zarrah seem to greatly benefit from having people around them who are willing to be open and talk about their sibling's death, including ministers, teachers, and counselors. Often, this kind of support is simply more available to rubber band teens, giving them a boost in both the short term and the long term as they cope with their loss, and perhaps making it easier for them to use this coping style. They also often have supportive family members, including extended family, who want to talk about the loss, making them feel more cared for. In some cases, these teens are fortunate to already have good problem-solving skills. To see how the old soul, replacement, and breakaway coping styles meld in the rubber band teen, let's take a closer look at Zarrah's story.

✳ Zarrah's Story

Zarrah's brother, Trey, a marine, was killed in Iraq while on active duty in Operation Iraqi Freedom. Trey, who had joined the military at age eighteen, died at age twenty during his second deployment when the Humvee he was traveling in hit a roadside bomb.

Most of Trey's friends had enlisted in the marines as soon as they were old enough, and many served alongside Trey. Some didn't survive the first deployment, like Trey's friend Lyle, who was taken hostage and killed. Losing Lyle had been really hard on Trey. They were the same age and had grown up together, so they'd always been in the same classes and usually walked to school and back home together.

The first time Trey deployed, Zarrah was twelve. He was gone for an entire year, but he kept in touch and sent her letters and pictures. Zarrah's friends at school told her how cute Trey looked posing with his gun in front of his Humvee. Zarrah continued to live her life the way she always had while Trey was gone, spending time with friends and family and playing sports. When Trey came home, he brought back souvenirs, along with lots of stories about the children he met in Iraq. Zarrah loved listening to his tales and asked lots of questions. She shared his answers about life in Iraq with her friends at school.

Although Trey was living with his girlfriend, Mary, while stateside, he spent a lot of time with Zarrah and his parents and made a point of coming over for dinner every Sunday, where he and Zarrah shared goofy looks and inside jokes at the dinner table like they always had. By the time Trey left for his second deployment, Mary was pregnant, and she was so upset that he had to leave.

Despite the fact that Trey's friend Luke had been killed in their first deployment, Zarrah couldn't imagine anyone being able to hurt her brother. She truly believed that if anyone tried to kill Trey, he'd be able to find a way to escape. She never doubted that he would come back home. But four months into his second deployment, Trey died in an instant. Nobody in the Humvee survived, and nobody could have known about the bomb. Trey was buried at Arlington National Cemetery. His girlfriend, Mary, was too upset to attend. The church arranged for several buses to take everyone to the burial. Zarrah's mother cried throughout the funeral but held her head high as she heard how brave her son was. Zarrah felt proud and held her head high too. The local paper even had an article about Trey, accompanied by a picture of him in his uniform. He looked serious but had a smile in his eyes. The caption read, "Local boy killed in Iraq. Nation mourns another hero."

Zarrah was devastated by Trey's death. She kept the newspaper, all of Trey's letters, and many pictures of Trey in a scrapbook. She called it her "Hero Book." After Trey's son, Trey Jr., was born, Zarrah added pictures of the baby to the book. The family vowed to keep Trey's memory alive by telling Trey Jr. what a brave man his father had been. They also planted a tree in his honor in their yard. Zarrah often sat beneath the tree with Trey Jr. Sometimes she looked through the scrapbook, sometimes she cried, and sometimes she talked to Trey and told him how much she missed him. She wished he could be there for her prom, for her first day of college, and to scare off boys. Yet she was comforted by her beliefs that he died for a greater purpose and that, in one way or another, he'd always be watching over her.

When she felt ready, Zarrah shared Trey's story with her friends at school. They asked a lot of questions. Some were more concrete, like "Why wasn't the Humvee protected better?" Some were more personal, like "How can you go on with your life?" While Zarrah sometimes felt like the odd one out, she sensed that her friends cared about her, even though they didn't understand what it was like to be in the middle of so much pain and loss. She also felt like she had a new sense of purpose—that it was her job to make sure everyone knew about her heroic brother. She brought her "Hero Book" to school and did a presentation on having a brother or sister who served in the military. Online, she reached out to other kids who had experienced similar losses and encouraged them to tell their sibling's story. Slowly, she developed into a newer version of herself: a proud surviving sibling.

Can You Relate to Zarrah?

Let's take a look at a few specific aspects of Zarrah's experience that you may relate to.

Zarrah felt like the community cared about her loss. Because Trey was a veteran, people in her community were saddened by his death. They reached out to her family and wanted to celebrate Trey too. And because Lyle had also died overseas, many people in the community were already familiar with this kind of loss. This helped Zarrah feel less isolated and alone in her grief. The newspaper called Trey a hero, and the family's church arranged for many people to attend his burial. As a result, Zarrah felt supported by more people than just her family, who were all grieving in their own ways.

Ask yourself: Are you part of a community that you feel cares for you, your sibling, and your family? Have people reached out and offered practical help, like meals or rides to school, or just to talk? When someone dies in service or of an illness, people in the community are often more willing to help and provide support. Unfortunately, when people commit suicide or are murdered, people may be more judgmental and less likely to help out.

Zarrah didn't have a lot of details about her brother's death. Zarrah knew Trey's Humvee hit a bomb and that he was killed instantly, so he didn't suffer. Because she didn't physically witness his death and heard about it secondhand, this may have made it easier for her to cope in healthier ways—in contrast to Tommy, in chapter 7, who saw his sister's body being carried away after she was killed in a hit-and-run accident. Other factors may also have helped Zarrah cope, including her outgoing personality and her recent experience with Lyle's death. In addition, she felt connected to Trey in many different ways, including through his son and in the letters he'd sent.

Ask yourself: Did you hear many details of your sibling's death or witness it, or do you wish you had more information about it? Do you have an especially vivid imagination that's made it hard for you to stop thinking about the death itself? Or, with time, have you been able to focus more on happier memories of your sibling? Was your sibling old enough for the two of you to have a relationship, or was he or she too little for you to really get to know? Do you feel that you have a personality that bounces back from hard events, or does it take you quite a while to feel better when bad things happen? Any of these factors can contribute to how you cope.

Zarrah searched for ways to create meaning from Trey's death. Of course, Zarrah felt sad, confused, and lonely at times, but she also worked on finding meaning in Trey's death. She was surrounded by people who cared about Trey, and all responded to his death in different ways: from Mary, who was too upset to attend Trey's funeral; to Zarrah's mother, who was generally able to feel proud of Trey despite her grief; to Zarrah's friends, who didn't fully understand what had happened but tried to talk to her about Trey and how she was feeling. All of these different reactions allowed Zarrah to experience many different types of feelings—not just sadness and dismay, but also hope and a sense of meaning.

Ask yourself: How have you responded to the different types of grief you see around you? For example, does the way your parents or caregivers grieve impact your own feelings about losing your brother or sister? Are there certain people in your life who might be more open to talking with you about your feelings, and do you feel comfortable seeking them out? Have you thought about how to live the rest of your life without your sibling and how you'll cope with the years ahead?

Things You Might Be Thinking

If you're a rubber band teen, you may have some of the common thoughts listed below. For each, I've provided an example to make it more concrete:

* *This really hurts for me and my family.*

   Reagan, seventeen: "My little sister's death meant the end of so many exciting things in my family's life. She was just a toddler, and she was so cute. It was fun getting to know the person she was becoming. All of a sudden her life was cut short. There aren't words to describe the pain we all feel, and we spend a lot of time crying."

* *Why did this have to happen?*

   Arnold, age fourteen: "I keep asking God *why*: 'Why did you have to take my brother away from us?' I feel like if there were some kind of reason or explanation, maybe we could all move forward. But

I don't know, maybe that wouldn't help, since he'd still be gone."

✳ *I want to tell my story.*

Elan, age fifteen: "I want people to know what happened so they can understand. I've always been a pretty talkative person, and I'm just not going to be quiet about my brother's death. People pretend it didn't happen or treat me like I'm different somehow. If they know—if I can explain it to them—maybe they can understand what it's like for me and other kids who lose a brother or sister."

✳ *It's hard to know who to talk to about this.*

Sonja, age sixteen: "We're a pretty close family, the six of us, but now one of us is missing and everybody is sad about it. My parents talk to our pastor, and my brothers have the school counselor. I guess I could talk to the school counselor too, but I feel funny talking to a stranger about our loss. Shouldn't the family be there for each other, rather than all of us talking to different people? Maybe somebody can help us work on doing that."

✳ *Time has helped, but it hasn't healed.*

Ingrid, age eighteen: "Five years have passed since my brother's suicide. I'll never understand why he did it, and sometimes I'm still so mad at him. But as time has gone on, I've learned how to live with my anger toward him and now I'm starting to think about happier memories too. I still have bad days when I think I'll never be able to forgive him, or myself for not stopping him, but there are more good days now."

✳ *Who am I now that I don't have a sibling?*

Ryker, age thirteen: "Everybody knew me as Bron's little brother. Now that Bron is gone and I'm going to start high school soon, I want to know: Who am I if I'm not Bron's little brother? Can I still be somebody's little brother if he isn't alive?"

Things You Might Be Doing

Certain behaviors are more common among rubber band teens. Read through the behaviors below and the example for each. Are you doing any of these things?

✳ Looking for people who get it

Elan has been searching for online support groups for teens who have lost a sibling. He wants to tell his story, but he also wants to talk to other teens who have gone through what he has.

✳ Trying to figure it all out

Ryker is confused: If his brother is dead, can he still be somebody's little brother? He always saw himself as the kid brother, and he enjoyed having Bron watch out for him. Now that Bron isn't around, Ryker is trying

*to figure out what life will look like from now on. He's
scared and worried, and sometimes he has trouble
sleeping. He's started talking to Bron's best friend,
Manny, about it, because he feels like Manny knew Bron
best. Talking to Manny helps Ryker feel connected to
Bron, and it's also made him realize that Manny has
always seen him as somebody with a personality all his
own, not just as Bron's little brother.*

✱ Looking toward the future

*Reagan was just getting used to being a big sister,
and now she's having to focus on how to cope as she
moves forward, instead. She'd like to learn how to carry
memories of her little sister and memorialize her. Her
family is planning to go to family therapy, and Reagan
is looking forward to getting started and hoping this will
help everyone deal with the pain of their loss.*

✱ Distracting yourself with enjoyable activities

*Ingrid has good days and bad days. When she's feeling
especially angry at her brother, she writes poems in her
journal, paints, or goes for a jog with her dog. Sometimes
she feels guilty about distracting herself, but she's also
come to realize that if she holds her anger in and focuses
on it without releasing it in healthy activities, she might
never be able move on in life. She hopes her brother
would want her to have some fun, but it has only been
in the past year that she has given herself permission to
have a good time again.*

The Challenge of Being a Rubber Band Teen

You've probably experienced a lot of different emotions since your brother or sister died. You may feel as though some days are good, some days are bad, and some are in between. At times, you may use the coping styles in the previous chapters. Perhaps you sometimes feel singled out or like a misfit, like a breakaway teen (chapter 7). Other times you may feel the need to take on more responsibilities to help your family, like teens who are old souls (chapter 5), or you may try to fill your sibling's shoes, like a replacement (chapter 6). And sometimes you may fantasize about escaping altogether.

On the whole, though, despite your feelings of loss, confusion, and even isolation, you probably seem to be coping very well—especially from the outside. For this reason, people who might be helpful to you right now, such as teachers, family members, and friends, might forget that you could still benefit from support and extra care and consideration. You might have thought of yourself as a self-starter in the past, and maybe you still are. Maybe you're able to ask for help when you need it or have been finding ways to help yourself through your grief, but maybe not. There's no need to hide your emotions or force yourself to move forward if you aren't ready.

Other Coping Styles You Might Relate To

I encourage you to read chapters 5 (on the old soul), 6 (on trying to replace your sibling), and 7 (on breakaway teens) if you haven't already. As a rubber band teen, your coping style may include elements of any of these others. It's likely that you'll find stories and examples in those chapters that reflect your experience, at least a bit.

What You Can Do About It

In part 3 of the book, you'll find many tools, tips, and exercises to help you on your journey toward healing:

* Chapter 10, "Don't Believe Everything You Think," will help you explore the thoughts and feelings that have come up for you as a result of your grief and how they've influenced your behaviors. If you're a rubber band, you may be coping fairly well already. Still, you'll find many tips and ideas in chapter 11 for reframing thoughts that may be pitfalls or distractions on your journey toward healing.

* Chapter 11, "Telling Your Story," has suggestions for a variety of creative ways to capture your voice as you consider sharing the story of your loss with others. Telling your story is one method of honoring your sibling while staying true to your own experience.

* Even if you feel that you're doing okay in facing your loss, dealing with life, and looking toward the future, your grief may still be overwhelming at times. Chapter 12 can help you normalize those feelings and work toward communicating your needs to others when you're feeling down or upset.

Concluding Thoughts

Many teens who have lost a sibling have a rubber band coping style. Sure, they have feelings of deep sadness and sometimes feel isolated. They may also sometimes face challenges in relationships with family members and friends. Yet in the long run, most teens do okay as they integrate the loss of a sibling into their life. Hopefully this chapter has bolstered your sense of strength and confidence in your ability to cope. You may also feel less alone now that you know it's most common for teens to have a rubber band coping style. And remember, wherever you are in your grief process, you probably won't be there forever.

Even if this chapter didn't bring up strong thoughts or feelings, consider taking some time to write in your journal or on the worksheet available online (at http://www.newharbinger .com/32493) about whatever did come up. Even though you may be mostly coping well, it's helpful just to have an outlet for your thoughts and feelings, including those that arise as you process what you've read in this chapter.

Part 3

Working Toward Healing

chapter 9

Taking a Breath

Whether you've recently lost your sibling or some time has passed, it's important to find tools that will help you cope and have a sense of control over your life. For most people, the feeling of loss of control seems to be one of the most powerful effects of losing a loved one. You might be thinking, *The world is no longer a safe place* or *The future scares me*. These kinds of thoughts can be overwhelming because they often feel so immediate and true, especially when you've had the devastating experience of losing someone in your life who you may have believed would always be there. The death of a brother or sister can shake anyone to the core.

Breaking the Cycle of Negative Thoughts and Feelings

Unfortunately, some of the things we tell ourselves about how life is or how it will be from now on aren't always helpful. And some of them can keep a grieving person in a cycle of isolation, sadness, anxiety, frustration, and other difficult feelings. The good news is, you can work with these thoughts and develop

alternatives that will help you cope better and feel more positive about the future.

In the aftermath of your loss, you may be asking, *Who am I?*
It's an important question (and, as mentioned, one all teens are
asking, to some extent). Just keep in mind that who you are can
change over time. And even though it may feel hard to believe
it right now, there are many ways you can work toward enjoying life and being excited about the future again. Sometimes
surviving siblings feel that if they experience any positive emotions, like joy and hope, they're letting their sibling down or
disrespecting his or her memory. However, there are ways to
feel good and take steps toward a happier and more productive
life without leaving your sibling behind, and this is probably
what your sibling would want for you. Moving forward doesn't
mean forgetting where you came from. To help you get started,
this short chapter offers a simple but very effective exercise that
you can do anytime, anywhere: Focusing on Breathing.

Exercise: Focusing on Breathing

Most of us don't focus on our breathing from moment to moment, and
the truth is, that's a good thing. Our bodies attend to breathing for us so
we can focus on living our lives. However, there are times when it can
be helpful to focus on your breathing and even try to reset it, especially if
you find yourself feeling anxious, overwhelmed, or even short of breath.
Learning how to focus on your breath can help you feel more calm and
comfortable when something triggers you or you're facing a difficult situation. Another good time to focus on breathing is before starting any
important task, including working on healing from your loss. In this exercise, you'll learn to use your breath to help you feel more calm and cen-

tered. I encourage you to practice this exercise at least once a day, and to set a goal of making it a regular part of your life.

Sit comfortably in a safe space—a place where you feel free to be yourself and relax, such as your bedroom. Begin by taking a slow, deep breath through your nose for at least three counts. Don't let your shoulders scrunch up or your chest rise really high. Instead, let your breath fill your belly and expand it. Think, Low and slow, as if you're gathering in a big, deep breath to inflate a balloon. If it helps, close your eyes and imagine your belly filling with warm, moist air. At the end of the third count, pause and briefly hold your breath. Then, even more slowly, exhale through your mouth for one count longer than your inhalation (usually four counts). Purse your lips in a slight O and allow all of the air to escape from your belly. Picture the air that's leaving your mouth as cool and icy, as if you're breathing out frosty winter air. Pause for one count at the end of the exhalation. You can take the visualization as far as you want, for example, picturing your breath creating icicles on tree branches. Repeat for at least three more breaths.

If you like, you can use music to help calm you, as long as it's quiet and instrumental and not distracting. The goal is to create a place of silence and stillness both inside your mind and in your surroundings. Don't worry if you lose focus or if your mind wanders as you do your breathing; that's normal. In time, with practice, it will probably happen less often. And if thoughts arise, don't judge yourself or the thoughts, whatever they may be. Just notice them and return your focus to your breath.

If you enjoy this exercise, feel free to practice longer or more often. If, on the other hand, you find it hard to focus and practice on your own, you can search online for downloadable audio instructions for mindful breathing—or even guided imagery, where you're invited to imagine yourself in different relaxing environments, such as a cool autumn forest or on a warm beach listening to the sounds of waves.

Concluding Thoughts

You've lost someone you love—someone you probably have lots of thoughts and feelings about. There's an absence in your life where somebody important used to be. And as you've learned, grief is a cyclical process, with days that are better and days that are harder. The remaining chapters in this book provide tools and techniques that can help you have more good days and keep making headway on your journey toward healing. But it won't happen all at once, and you'll still have tough times. Wherever you are—now and in any given moment—tell yourself, *This is where I am right now, and it's not forever.*

It's going to take time for some of the strategies in part 3 of the book to start working. It won't always feel easier, but there are ways to explore your feelings and know they're okay—and that you'll be okay too. So maybe take a minute now to repeat the breathing exercise in this chapter. Then, when you're ready, turn to chapter 10, where you'll start working with your thoughts and feelings.

chapter 10

Don't Believe
Everything You Think

Would you agree that no two people have the exact same way of looking at the world? If you aren't sure, try this: Imagine yourself lying in the grass with a friend, looking at clouds in the sky. Perhaps a particularly puffy one floats by that reminds you of Santa Claus's head, complete with a big white beard. As you look at the cloud with the idea of Santa in your mind, you may start finding even more examples of how the cloud looks just like him, perhaps the twirl of his mustache or the chubby apple of his cheek. But what about your friend? Maybe your friend can't see Santa Claus in the cloud, despite the image being so clear to you. Maybe, instead, she insists that the cloud looks like a duck swimming through water. Perhaps she even tries to point out the way the wings of the duck rest against its body, or the curve of its beak, but you still can't see it.

This is a very concrete example of how each of us lives in a world shaped by how we see and interpret things. You look at the world through your own lenses. Nobody else can be inside your head, and you can't be inside anyone else's head either. And, importantly, just because you see something a certain way, that doesn't mean what you see is definitely reality.

The Inner Voice

We all fall victim to listening to an inner voice that tells us stories about *everything*. This voice in your head, the voice of your own thoughts, likes to narrate. It tells stories, judges, observes, explores, and tries to explain things. Because the voice in your head is uniquely you, it's hard not to listen to it and think it's always right. But what if the voice in your head is sometimes a little judgmental, unforgiving, or just plain wrong about things? This is something worth exploring.

Exercise: Noticing When the Voice Got It Wrong

The first big question is whether the voice in your head is always right, or if it needs to brush up on reality a bit. Take a minute now to remember a time when that inner voice had you convinced of something that turned out to be untrue. Once you've called a situation to mind, get out your journal or the worksheet available at http://www.newharbinger .com/32493 and write your answers to these questions:

- **The trigger:** What caused or led up to the event?

- **Your thoughts at the time:** What did the voice in your head say?

- **Your feelings at the time:** What emotions did you feel, based on the thoughts you had?

- **What you did because of how you thought and felt:** Did you take any action because of how you were feeling and thinking?

- **What actually happened:** How did the voice get it wrong?

Here's an example from Becca, the old soul in chapter 5, to get you started:

- **The trigger:** *I left the laundry in the washing machine overnight, and it smelled really awful. I had to wash it again in the morning, and because of that, my dad didn't have any clean socks and had to wear an old pair with holes in the toes.*

- **My thoughts at the time:** *The voice in my head told me, "You're so stupid. You're so careless. Your dad is going to have a bad day because of you. And if he can't trust you to do the laundry right, how can he trust you at all?"*

- **My feelings at the time:** *I felt sick to my stomach and so mad at myself that I wanted to punch something. Then I got really sad because if Joseph were still alive my mom wouldn't be out of commission and would be able to do the laundry. Then I felt guilty for another thought that came— that my mom was lazy.*

- **What I did:** *I started to cry, and I hit the washing machine with my hand because I was embarrassed about crying. I was late for school because I felt like I couldn't get myself under control. I also avoided my dad because I was afraid he'd yell at me.*

- **What actually happened:** *My dad came downstairs with his toe sticking out of his sock, and it was actually pretty funny. He wiggled it at me and made it have a super geeky voice. It was so lame that I started to laugh. He told me it was okay that I messed up the wash and that I shouldn't be so hard on myself. I was so sure he was going to be mad at me, but everything was okay. I wish I hadn't gotten so caught up with the voice in my head.*

As you can see from Becca's example, she was convinced that she'd ruined her father's day. Her thoughts went down a slippery slope toward sadness and guilt, causing her to feel even worse. But her thoughts were distorted; they weren't based in reality, and what ended up happening wasn't nearly as bad as what she feared would happen.

Now that you've seen that example, give the exercise a try yourself. Once you get started, you may be able to think of quite a few times when the voice in your head was pretty convincing about predictions of the future that didn't actually come true. You can do this exercise for as many of them as you like, or just make a list of them.

The Link Between Thoughts, Feelings, and Actions

When you did the preceding exercise, you may have noticed that it's pretty hard to not listen to that voice in your head. And that's actually a good thing. You need to have a place inside yourself where you can explore, explain, mull over, make decisions, and react to the world around you. Still, that inner voice can be critical, mean, and pretty unhelpful at times, yet it's hard to ignore it. And even worse, as you now know, that inner voice isn't always right.

There are all kinds of reasons why thoughts become distorted. One is that certain ways of thinking can be passed down in your family. That was the case for Tommy, from chapter 7. As he put it, "My mother always told us not to step on cracks in the sidewalk because it would cause something bad to happen to you. And one time, when I broke a mirror, she said that meant we'd have seven years of bad luck. When Isla died, I seriously wondered if it was because of the broken mirror." Tommy's mother is superstitious, and he's learned some of her ways of thinking about the world.

Another way thoughts can become distorted is when important people in your life convey messages about how you should act in various situations. This was the case for Eric, from chapter 6: "The school principal told me I had to be a good example to everyone because Luke had been such a good example. I understood that a good kid is supposed to fill his dead brother's shoes, so I felt like I didn't have a choice about it." To Eric, it seems that he's expected to act a certain way, and he doesn't feel like he has other options.

It can be really tough to feel like you have to act a certain way all the time, rather than just being yourself. To make things even more complicated, how you think can affect how you feel, and ultimately, both can affect the decisions you make about how to act in the world—something you probably noticed when you did the previous exercise. Let's take a look at how that worked for Tommy and Eric, tracing the links between their thoughts, feelings, and actions. As you'll see, actions can just continue the cycle:

Tommy

Thought: *I broke the mirror and brought bad luck onto my family. It's my fault Isla is dead.*

Feelings: *I feel guilty, embarrassed, ashamed, and responsible.*

Action: *Since I'm no good, I might as well go out and get into more trouble, breaking more things, drinking, and doing drugs.*

Thought: *Nothing will ever get better for me. I'm doomed.*

Eric

Thought: *I need to live up to Luke's legacy because everybody expects that from me.*

Feelings: *I feel lonely and worthless.*

Action: *I'll do everything Luke did. I'll even wear his clothes to be more like him.*

Thought: *I don't know who I am anymore. Nobody cares about me. They all just want Luke.*

Can you see that both Tommy and Eric ended up having thoughts that kept them trapped in a cycle that made them feel even worse about themselves? It wouldn't be surprising if they took further actions based on those upsetting feelings.

For Tommy and Eric, and maybe for you too, the inner voice can lead to negative feelings and maybe even unhealthy decisions. Your thoughts can influence how you feel and what you do about it, locking you into a cycle of beating up on yourself, and sometimes separating you from people in your life who want to help.

Exercise: Making the Link

Take a moment now and think of a time when you got stuck in a pattern of unhelpful thoughts. Then, just as I did above for Tommy and Eric, write out a list showing the connections. In your journal, describe your own cycle with these elements. (A worksheet is also available at http://www.newharbinger.com/32493, if that's more convenient for you.)

Thought: Write down a thought you had that was triggered by how you felt you should have acted in a situation, based on others' expectations or even your own.

Feelings: Write down how you felt as a result of this thought. Don't describe the feeling; name it. This will help you identify the feeling itself, rather than describing the thought behind the feeling.

Action: Write down any actions you took or decisions you made because of the way you were feeling.

Thought: Write down a thought that arose because of how you acted.

Here's one more example, this time from Becca, to get you started.

Thought: *I should have stayed home the night of Joseph's suicide. If I had stayed home, I could have stopped him from killing himself.*

Feelings: *I feel guilty, hopeless, and ashamed, and I blame myself.*

Action: *I need to make sure I'm home all the time now to take care of everybody else in my life. I need to protect them the way I couldn't protect Joseph.*

Thought: *I'm trapped. I'll never be able to leave the house or live my own life again.*

When you're ready, give it a try with the example you came up with at the start of this exercise. Can you see how your thoughts, feelings, and actions are interrelated? Can you think of other examples? Take your time with this exercise and consider how this plays out in your life so you can really start to see the links between thinking, feeling, doing, and thinking again. Then we'll take a look at how you can break the cycle.

Breaking the Cycle: Changing How You Feel Based on How You Think

The previous exercise may have made you feel overwhelmed or frustrated, or it may have brought up other strong emotions.

It can be pretty eye-opening to see how your patterns of thinking may be affecting your emotions and the decisions you make, especially if this is happening on an ongoing basis. Don't despair! There are some simple, effective ways to break cycles of thoughts and feelings that leave you feeling trapped, helpless, or hopeless. Here's the key: you need to be ready to do battle with the voice in your head. We'll start to work on that shortly, but first, here are a few tips for preparing to wage war on unhelpful thoughts.

Focus on the Here and Now

Sometimes we believe what the inner voice tells us because of experiences we've lived through in the past. Because you've lost a sibling, it's natural and normal to look back and try to find an explanation for why things happened the way they did. The problem is, it's easy to place too much emphasis on hindsight and find patterns where none actually exist—especially when it comes to doubt, blame, guilt, and shame. It usually isn't helpful to focus on past events and use them to try to predict how you're going to act in the future. After all, you don't have a crystal ball, and there are many factors involved in any situation or life event. So if you find yourself focusing on the past or, at the other extreme, worrying about the future, take a deep breath and try to stay in the present. Focusing on the here and now will allow you to tackle the thoughts that are going through your head in the moment and help you come up with a plan for how to work with them or change them.

Understand That Change Is an Ongoing Process

True transformation and the path to healing begin when you're ready to confront your thoughts and try to find new ways to interpret events and your life and relationships. But this can't happen all at once. It takes time and practice to learn not to rely on your gut instincts, and it can be hard not to fall back on old patterns that can keep you locked into unhealthy emotions, especially when life is stressful. Change can be frightening and overwhelming, and sometimes it feels easier to stay stuck, even if you don't like where you are.

Go easy on yourself and don't expect to change or feel better all at once. There will be moments when you feel better and others when you feel worse. Don't give up when you feel down. Sit with your feelings and praise yourself for being willing to work toward healing. Also tell yourself, *This won't last forever.* Just as it takes time and practice to learn new skills, like playing a musical instrument or mastering a new language, it takes time for your brain to acquire new ways of thinking.

Look for Tools to Help You

As you learn to confront the voice in your head, you may find it helpful to write in your journal. This can be a way of moving your thoughts from inside your head onto paper. It can also help you track your progress. As one part of your writing, consider doing the exercises in this chapter time and time again, and reward yourself with a fun activity each time you do.

When you're ready, it might also be a good idea to look for teen grief support groups in your area. Other outside sources of support include professionals, such as a counselor or social worker, or a trusted mentor, family friend, or clergyperson. Connecting with any of these sources of support will give you more opportunities to talk about your grief and the work you're doing to cope with it. The more support you have, whether it's coming from recording your progress in a journal or cheerleaders in your everyday life, the easier it will be to stay on track with the healing process.

Check In with Your Body

Your body can be a great source of information. Among other things, it can tell you if you're grounded in anxiety or reality. Here's a fun technique to get more in tune with your body. Set a timer for one minute. Then, during that minute, try to focus on your heartbeat without checking for your pulse. Close your eyes and count how many times your heart beats just by paying attention to the feeling of your heart as it works in your body. When the minute is up, write down the number of beats you perceived. Next, press two fingers against the inside of your wrist or on your neck just out from your throat—wherever you can feel your pulse best. Then once again set the timer for one minute and count how many times your heart beats by observing your pulse. Write that number down too.

What do you notice? Were your numbers close together or far apart? Did you count more beats when you weren't using your pulse? If that's the case, you might be experiencing some anxiety. Your mind might be telling you that your heart is beating faster than usual, creating symptoms like panic and fear, when your heart may, in fact, be beating at a normal rate. This is a great exercise for developing more awareness about how in tune you are with your body versus how much you might be stuck in your head.

If you found that you overestimated how quickly your heart was beating, or if you simply discovered that you *are* feeling anxious, it may be useful for you to return to the breathing exercise in chapter 9. It will help you slow your breathing down, which will calm your mind. Also note that the more often you do that breathing practice, especially if you do it when you aren't feeling anxious, the easier it will be for you to go into a calmer zone of deep breathing when you're feeling overwhelmed.

Look for Other Ways to Separate Fact from Fiction

Like a reporter doing research for a story, try to explore what the real world looks like by seeking out just the facts of a situation and not attaching emotions to them. Look at all sides of an issue, not just yours or the one you can relate to the most. As you've been learning, your own thoughts aren't always reliable, so it's important to collect facts from lots of different sources. Explore your situation from the point of view of others in your life, and question every assumption you make. Ask yourself, *Do I have proof that stands behind this conclusion, or are my emotions clouding the situation?* Most importantly, look for times when the voice in your head might be steering you toward making assumptions that aren't exactly accurate. If you aren't sure how to do that, no problem. Just read on!

Identifying Distortions in Your Thought Process

The preceding tips will help you begin to challenge your thoughts. But how exactly do you do that? First, it's important to recognize the many ways in which thoughts can be deceiving or how they can be distorted, just like a fun-house mirror that warps your reflection. In the sections that follow, I'll describe some of the most common tricks the inner voice can use to distort our interpretations of reality, and how we can fight back.

Black-and-White Thinking

Do you ever get stuck looking at the world in extremes? To see how this looks in real life, consider Tommy, from chapter 7. When he was first arrested, he thought, *I'm a terrible person. I'm no good and things will never get better.* This is an example of black-and-white thinking. For Tommy, there's no gray area, no in-between. His thought process has him convinced that if he isn't 100 percent good, he's 100 percent terrible. Yet an outsider looking at Tommy's situation might find it easier to challenge his reasoning. In fact, it's probably easy for you to argue with it. Perhaps you might tell Tommy, "Nobody is completely bad. There are lots of reasons why people get into trouble or do bad things."

How to fight it: Of course, it's much harder to challenge black-and-white thinking when it's happening inside your own head. So you might start by looking at examples where other people are thinking in extremes. After practicing that for a while, you may be able to more often see that reality isn't as cut-and-dried as your thoughts may sometimes make it out to be.

Crystal Ball Gazing

Do you have the power to foresee the future? While many of us wish we had this gift, we simply don't have that capability. Yet for some reason, the inner voice can convince us that we're able to know the outcome of most situations in advance. Let's take another look at the example from Becca, earlier in this chapter, about fouling up the laundry. Becca was convinced that not having clean socks would ruin her father's day. Worrying about it made her feel worse. What ended up happening was different. If Becca had seen her prediction as just being a thought inside her head, she might have more easily seen that she can't predict what will happen.

How to fight it: When your thoughts try to convince you that the outcome of a situation will be terrible, remember that it's impossible to predict the future, especially based on past events. Just because something painful happened in the past, that doesn't mean the same thing is guaranteed to happen again. The truth is, there's no way of knowing what the future will bring, especially in situations where multiple people, expectations, and events are involved. By the way, another thing human beings are incapable of doing is reading minds. So try not to predict what others are going to say to you or think about you, because there's simply no way to know for sure.

Overgeneralizing

Are you the type of person who makes overgeneralizations? For a real-life example of this, consider Eric's thought in response to the principal's decree that he should fill his brother's shoes: *Nobody cares about me. They all just want Luke.* This powerful overgeneralization influenced Eric to the point that he abandoned his own hopes and dreams and instead tried to become more like Luke in every way.

How to fight it: When you overgeneralize, you neglect important details, facts, and contradictory evidence that make situations unique and complex. In Eric's case, you might argue, "The school principal wants you to be a role model like your brother, but that doesn't mean you have to be exactly like Luke in every way. People miss your brother, but that doesn't mean they don't want you around. You are your own person. Plus, the principal is just one person; he doesn't speak for everyone." When you find yourself overgeneralizing, try to look into the details of the situation. Also remember where other people are coming from and that their view of the world is different from yours. One good way to fight any tendency to overgeneralize is to think of times in your life when you thought this way and missed out on important details.

Catastrophizing

After a brother or sister dies, it's a normal reaction to see the world as a place that is no longer safe and think life can be very unpredictable. The problem is, if you start looking at life through this lens a lot of the time, you'll miss many chances to see the wonderful opportunities, relationships, and events that surround you every day. The world is a complex place to live in, and it isn't all good or all bad. Yet after tragedy strikes, people sometimes feel the need to protect themselves by planning for the worst. This is called catastrophizing, meaning you expect things to end in disaster. After Isla died, Tommy felt this way. He told his school counselor: "I'll never feel safe again. Every time I cross the street, I'm sure a car will swing around out of nowhere and hit me. When we went on vacation to Disney World last month with my cousins, I was sure the plane was going to crash. I didn't want to get on. They had to force me, and I was panicking the whole flight." As you might expect, Tommy's belief that disasters lurk around every corner can really limit his life, keeping him caged in fear. Or when he's feeling low, his sense that he's helpless and life is out of control can trigger him to engage in behaviors that are extreme and dangerous, like riding his bike across traffic. Somewhere in the back of his mind, he may be thinking, *If disaster is inevitable, what does it matter?*

How to fight it: Bad things do happen. You know this firsthand. But that doesn't mean every situation is going to end in disaster. Try to think of a time in your life when you were afraid something bad would happen and it didn't. As a rule, bad events are highlighted in our memories, which makes them seem more common than they actually are. One way to catastrophize when a loved one dies is to fear dying in the same way. This may be the case for you, especially if your brother or sister died of an illness or medical condition. This is an understandable fear, but keep in mind that most of the time our bodies work properly and help us live and thrive. So take a moment to say thank you to your body for working properly: thank your lungs for breathing, thank your brain for helping you read these words, and thank the muscles that allow you to stretch and be flexible.

Coming Down with a Case of the "Shoulds"

Over the course of your life, you've probably heard many messages from friends, family members, teachers, and others about how you're expected to think, feel, or act in a variety of situations. Those messages can take up residence in your head and become very absolute and unforgiving, showing up as a voice that tells you how you should be behaving or feeling. While it's good to have some general rules to guide your behavior and interactions with others, there are no one-size-fits-all ways to be—not just because we're all different, but also because most situations are complex. You might get stuck in trying do what you believe you should in a particular moment and, in the process, lose track of your genuine self, including important feelings or reactions. That's what happened to Eric at his brother's funeral. As he described it, "I was so sad that Luke was gone. I felt like I'd lost a big piece of myself. I wanted to cry so badly, but I remembered what my grandfather said when Luke was sick: 'He'd want you to be happy. You should try to honor that.' My dad wasn't crying because he said men don't cry. So I felt like I had to ignore my feelings and act strong."

How to fight it: For Eric, the end result of abiding by "shoulds" was that he didn't feel he could express his sadness. What if he had? If Eric had cried, would the world have ended? Would his father or grandfather have been disappointed? Probably not. It's normal to express grief and cry when a loved one dies. When you come down with a case of the "shoulds," ask yourself where this prescription for behavior came from and whether it's helpful for you to follow it. Conduct a thought experiment: What if you ignored what you "should" do and instead focused on being true to yourself and your feelings? What's the worst that could happen? Are there some situations where it's okay to break with convention?

Magical Thinking

Young children often see the world as a magical place, where their thoughts and behaviors can control the environment around them. For example, a small child might believe that if she behaves well at dinner, she'll have sweet dreams when she goes to bed. Another small child might think he can control the weather if he concentrates very hard. As we grow up, we begin to understand that the world doesn't quite work this way—that we don't have all that much power when it comes to the world around us. However, the voice in your head might sometimes tell you otherwise. Take the example of Tommy and the broken mirror, from earlier in this chapter. Due to magical thinking, Tommy can't help but wonder if Isla's death is part of the seven years of bad luck his mother said the family would have.

How to fight it: Can Tommy really be responsible for Isla getting hit by a car? Is there any way breaking a mirror one day, in one location, can result in a drunk driver hitting a little girl at a different time in a completely different location? If magical thinking had any true power, imagine how many disasters would occur on a minute-by-minute basis as bad thoughts and superstitions controlled the world around us. As humans, we like to find reasons why bad things happen, and doing so can even be useful, but as we do so, we need to keep in mind that it's events, behaviors, and other external factors—not thoughts—that usually cause things to happen. So while it's common to consider whether having a bad thought can translate into seriously harming someone in real life, there are no scientific studies indicating that this is the case. As a teen, one of your greatest gifts, courtesy of developments in your brain, is the power to pick apart arguments and be critical. So try to be critical of superstitious and magical thinking.

Zooming In on the Bad, Zooming Out on the Good

Have you ever heard the expression that it's easy to kick someone when he's down? We do this to ourselves all the time, bullying ourselves mentally. When you're feeling bad about yourself, you might add to your emotional state by focusing only on negative, unhelpful areas of your life that reinforce the way you're feeling. You end up caging yourself in by not thinking about anything positive or happy in your life. To see how this plays out, consider Becca. At night in bed, she often feels isolated and alone and thinks nobody cares about her. When this happens, she starts exploring all the negatives in her life that point to the thought being true: *I'm not useful to others unless I'm helping out, but I suck at taking care of people. I couldn't take care of Joseph, and he committed suicide. That's just like the time when I was five and our pet hamster died because I forgot to feed it. I'm a failure.*

How to fight it: Becca is making assumptions about herself based on isolated events in her life. There have been moments when she's been unable to care for others, but she's currently doing a great deal to care for others, and doing so successfully. Plus, as a teenager, is taking care of others really her responsibility? If Becca were to paint a more balanced picture of herself, she wouldn't feel so much like a failure. When you find yourself focusing on the negatives, ask yourself, *Am I kicking myself when I'm down? Is the negative really all there is about me, or am I focusing on it because I feel so terrible? What are some positives about me that I'm ignoring right now?*

Calling Yourself Nasty Names

How many times have you told yourself, *I'm a loser, I'm a failure, I'm no good,* or a host of other insults? As with the mental bullying involved in zooming in on the bad, calling yourself hurtful, judgmental names is also a form of kicking yourself when you're down. In the example above, Becca called herself a failure, and of course that didn't help her feel better.

How to fight it: When you start applying unkind labels to yourself, ask yourself, *Is this helpful, or is it hurting me?* Really think about it: Where is name-calling getting you? If it isn't useful and keeps you stuck in a cycle of sadness, guilt, blame, and other unhelpful emotions, maybe it's time to give it a rest and stop calling yourself names. If you feel this is a hard part of you to control, try not to judge the names you give yourself or yourself for doing so. Instead, take an attitude of interest and curiosity, telling yourself something like *Hmm... This is interesting. I'm calling myself a bad name again. I must be feeling really bad about myself.* By separating yourself from the immediate pain name-calling creates and trying not to judge the process, you can help yourself start feeling better.

Exercise: Identifying and Challenging Distortions

Now that you've learned about some of the most common thought distortions that can get you into trouble, you can practice identifying them in your day-to-day life. Then you can challenge the distortions—the first step to coming up with new, substitute thoughts. Remember the exercise "Noticing When the Voice Got It Wrong," at the beginning of the chapter? This exercise is similar, asking you to think of specific examples of times when your thoughts led you to feel a certain way. But in this case, you'll make a point of choosing a situation in which your initial thought was clearly distorted. Try to tease apart the experience, noticing how your thoughts were distorted and what effects this had on you. Then take some time to consider how you could have looked at the situation differently. Here are some questions to guide you through the process. Jot down your answers in your journal or on the worksheet available online:

- What were you thinking?

- How did you feel based on what you were thinking?

- Did you have any proof that your thoughts were accurate, or could they have been distorted?

- How might your thoughts have been distorted?

- Were these thoughts helpful in making you feel better, or did they keep you stuck in unhelpful emotions?

- What's another way you could have looked at the situation?

- How might you have felt if you'd looked at the situation differently?

It's highly worthwhile to learn to identify distorted thoughts—and if you can do so when they're arising, all the better! Practice will help you do this more often, so you might want to repeat this exercise for a variety of different thoughts, doing it regularly over the next few weeks.

Exercise: Creating Substitute Thoughts

Now that you've learned how to identify distorted ways of thinking, the next step is working on substituting more accurate thoughts, which will generally be healthier for you. For this exercise, think of a recent event that brought up some distorted thinking that led you to feel bad and influenced what you did. Then, in your journal or using the worksheet at http://www.newharbinger.com/32493, write down, as honestly as possible, your thoughts, feelings, and what you may have done as a result. In case an example would be helpful, let's look at this process for Becca and her feelings of responsibility for Joseph's death. Here's what she thinks, feels, and does.

Think, Feel, Do

Think: *I wasn't home when Joseph died. I should have been there. I could have made a difference. I could have talked him down or done CPR.*

Feel: *Those thoughts made me feel hyperresponsible, super guilty, and also helpless and out of control. I feel like I want to throw up, and also like I want to cry.*

Do: *I wanted to make sure everyone else in my life was safe, because I had control over that. So I took care of my mom and dad, made sure I was home as much as I could be, and stopped spending time with my friends.*

Go ahead and do this part of the exercise in your journal before you read on.

Now look back at what you wrote. Can you see the links between your thoughts, feelings, and behaviors? If you can, you're ready to proceed to part 2 of this exercise: challenging the thought distortion that's influencing how you feel and act.

Thought Challenge!

Start by identifying the distortion in your thinking. If need be, use the previous exercise, "Identifying and Challenging Distortions." Go ahead and write down the distortion in your thinking, then examine it and, just like a lawyer in a courtroom, argue with it! Here are some questions to help you challenge your thought, along with examples of how Becca might respond.

- **What were you thinking?** *That I was responsible for Joseph's death.*

- **How did you feel based on what you were thinking?** *Hyperresponsible, super guilty, helpless, and out of control.*

- **Did you have any proof that your thoughts were accurate, or could they have been distorted?** *Other than what the voice in my head told me, I have no evidence to prove I could have helped stop Joseph's death or save him. My thought could be distorted.*

- **How might your thoughts have been distorted?** *This might be a case of jumping to conclusions. How was I supposed to know Joseph was going to kill himself that night?*

- **Were these thoughts helpful in making you feel better, or did they keep you stuck in unhelpful emotions?** *They kept me stuck and feeling guilty.*

- **What's another way you could have looked at the situation?** *Maybe I could tell myself that I was a good big sister and did everything I could to help Joseph, and that he didn't seem any different the day he died. I don't know what time he died, what his thoughts were, and if anything I could have done would have made a difference. That's a huge burden to put on myself. My mom was home and she couldn't stop it either. I'm not God. I can't control what other people do.*

- **How might you have felt if you'd looked at the situation differently?** *Maybe I wouldn't have blamed myself so much.*

If you haven't already, go ahead and challenge your thought just as Becca did, using the same questions and writing your replies in your journal.

Substitute New Thoughts

Next, you'll return to the process at the beginning of this exercise (Think, Feel, Do), but this time you'll modify your thought based on the second part of the exercise (Thought Challenge!). It can be helpful to use the word "But" to introduce your new thoughts. This expresses that they contrast with your old, unhelpful thought. After writing your new thoughts, you'll explore how they may affect what you feel and do next.

Think: *I wasn't home when Joseph killed himself and I feel like I could have stopped him. But that sounds like jumping to conclusions. Looking back, it's easy for me to say I could have changed the situation, but I had gone out when Joseph was at home many nights before, and he never tried to hurt himself. How was I supposed to know that this night was different when he was acting the same way as always?*

Feel: *I'm Joseph's big sister, not a superhero. I couldn't sacrifice my life to protect him all the time, and his choices were his own. I feel sad and I still feel a little guilty, but I think it's okay for me to not take 100 percent of the responsibility in this case.*

Do: *I'm going to keep writing my feelings out about this, and I'm also going to make a list of all the happy memories I have of Joseph. He was having a hard time, but I don't want his death to be the only thing I remember about him. We had a good relationship, and he used to tell me that he loved that I had lots* *of friends and had a fun life. I think he'd want me to still enjoy myself. I'm going to make more of an effort to spend time doing things I enjoy, but I'll keep trying to make sure my mom is doing okay. I'll also try to explain these thought distortions to my mom so she knows this isn't all her fault either.*

If you haven't already, go ahead and complete this part of the exercise, using your new, more accurate thoughts and seeing how they could influence how you feel and what you might do.

The key to feeling better is recognizing and challenging distorted thoughts. Each time you identify a thought that's keeping you stuck in an unhelpful cycle, wage war with it, starting with the word "but," which will encourage you to think of alternatives. Then write down all the evidence against the distorted thought and come up with a new, more accurate way of seeing the situation.

Finding Healthy Ways to Cope

As you work on identifying distorted thoughts and coming up with substitute thoughts that are more accurate, you may start feeling a little better. Still, your emotions may sometimes get the best of you and feel overwhelming. Here's a list of healthy ways to cope when that happens:

* **Breathe deeply.** The exercise in chapter 9 is a quick and simple way to calm strong emotions.

* **Write it out.** Write down everything that's going through your head. Don't worry about spelling, punctuation,

grammar, or neatness. Just let your thoughts flow onto the page in front of you.

* **Distract yourself.** When emotions get intense, it can be hard to remember strategies for distracting yourself. So, right now, make a list of some of your favorite distractions; examples might be "Get out of the house," "Listen to some music," "Get some chores done," or "Check my e-mail." You might even want to cut a piece of paper into several smaller pieces and write one strategy on each. Then fold them up and put them in a hat or other container. When you start feeling overwhelmed, all you have to do is reach in, grab one, and do it!

* **Reach out.** It can be hard to ask for help. You may think it's a sign of weakness, but truly, it's a sign of strength. The first step is to make a list of people you might be willing to reach out to when your thoughts or feelings get the best of you. You don't necessarily have to discuss your feelings with them, so don't let that limit who you might list. Possibilities include friends who make you laugh, a clergyperson who will pray with you, a grandparent who likes to chat, or even your pet. Get outside of your head by focusing on others and interacting with them.

* **Tense and release.** Sometimes we habitually carry so much stress and strain in our bodies that we aren't even aware of how tight our muscles are. When you start feeling overwhelmed, try balling your fingers into a fist, squeezing hard, and holding it for a second. Notice all the tension in your hand as the blood flow is temporarily constricted. Then release and shake your hand out and

notice the difference between a state of tension and a state of relaxation, You can do the same thing with your entire body, tensing and releasing each major muscle group in turn, to help you relax. The more you practice this, the more you'll notice when your body is feeling tense in day-to-day life.

* **Focus on your senses.** Describe all of the different sights, smells, sounds, and textures around you in as much detail as possible. For example, if you're sitting on your bed you might start with "The bed is soft. The bedspread has a checkered blue pattern. It feels a bit thin in places. The room is warm, but my window is open and a slight breeze is coming in. I'm hearing a lawnmower next door, but now it stops and everything seems so quiet. Oh, now I hear the clanking of dishs down in the kitchen. I'm looking at a poster on my wall. The surface is shiny. The poster is of..." Focusing on your senses is a quick and easy way to distract yourself from unhelpful thoughts.

Now that you have a few ideas to get you started, you might want to add to this list with some ideas of your own. In your journal, brainstorm about other ways you can get out of your head and start feeling better.

Self-Help in Practice: Success Stories

To give you a better idea how to use the strategies in this chapter in real life, let's take a look at how some other teens used them successfully.

✳ *Becca*

I was taking so much responsibility for Joseph's death, and I didn't realize that by blaming myself for Joseph's death, I was forcing myself into taking care of my entire family. I was living in a black-and-white world, telling myself I had to do every-thing to care for my family or I sucked, and I was definitely caught up in "shoulds," feeling I had no choice in the matter. As I began to explore my thought processes, I realized that there was room for some shades of gray. While I still have trouble letting go of the thought that I played a role in Joseph's death by not being home, I'm beginning to understand that it wasn't really about me at all, and it didn't happen just because I wasn't there. I'm only one person, and Joseph's death was complicated and involved a lot of factors.

I've tried to replace my guilty thoughts, like It's so unfair that Joseph killed himself, and I'm angry at him for doing it, *with healthier ones, like* But I tried as best as I knew how to help him. *I also ask myself whether it was really my job to look out for Joseph and remind myself that I'm not his mother, I'm his sister. I don't know that it's fair for one kid to feel com-pletely responsible for another. Recently I wrote Joseph a letter, just to share some of my thoughts and get them out of my head. I told him about how I'm sad and I'm sorry, and that I hope he's doing okay wherever he is. I hope I can share my letter with my dad. I also want to talk with my dad about ways to bring my mom back into our family.*

✳ *Tommy*

A lot of things are affecting my feelings about myself, and a lot of them have to do with how Isla died. It was hard for me to get help because my emotions felt so raw. It seemed easier to go out and drink or act crazy than face what happened to my sister and seeing her body being carried away from that awful scene. I've been doing a lot of tensing and releasing to relax my body. I'm also working on focusing on my breathing to help me calm down when my heart starts pounding and I feel like I'm flashing back to that day.

There are definitely a lot of distorted thoughts in my brain. I keep thinking that nobody can relate to me because of what happened, and when I try to argue with that thought, I realize that it's hard for people to ask me questions about Isla because the whole thing is so bad. I can think of times when bad things happened to other people and I wanted to ask questions or be there for them, but I kept my mouth shut because I didn't want to say the wrong thing and make it worse. I think that might be how some of my friends feel around me. Plus, guys don't really talk about this stuff anyway.

I also notice that I feel sad so much. I have a hard time handling sad feelings, so I act out, like those times when I'm the class clown and make it hard for my homeroom teacher. I'm not gonna lie; I like the way it feels when I have the other kids' attention and they laugh at me. But I know it's not helping my grades. I've been trying to think of ways to get attention that will help me feel good without making school harder.

It's also been helpful for me to challenge my thoughts about the broken mirror. The other day I drew a big pie chart and tried to do percentages: how much was the drunk driver responsible, how much was I responsible because of breaking the mirror, and even how much Isla was responsible for crossing the street. It was helpful to look at it like that and actually see that I'm not the only player in this game. But I do think I probably need to go to a therapist for more help. The flashbacks of what happened to Isla are still hitting me pretty hard, and that makes it harder for me to notice my distorted thinking and challenge my thoughts. Still, I'm glad I got started on it.

Concluding Thoughts

Congratulations on starting to take some active steps in working toward healing. This chapter provided a number of ways to explore your thoughts, feelings, and actions as you cope with your grief. At first it can be challenging to identify thought processes that may be keeping you stuck in painful emotions or unhealthy patterns of behavior, but with time it will get easier. Just keep working on identifying and challenging distorted thoughts. If it's helpful, you can use the worksheet available at http://www.newharbinger.com/32493 to reflect on what you read, learned, and tried in this chapter. And remember, when it comes to working with your thoughts, consistent practice is the key. Find some time every day to reflect upon moments that felt painful or overwhelming and write about them in your journal, exploring whether these experiences were caused by unhelpful ways of thinking. By making this part of your daily routine, you'll be dedicating part of your day to working toward feeling healthier and happier. You'll also be learning to devote some time to taking care of yourself—something well worth doing! Although it can be hard work, I promise that you can only benefit from doing it. And it will get easier with time.

chapter 11

Telling Your Story

Each of us sees the world in a different way, and every single human being has a story to tell about it. And while we all have an inner voice that's doing its best to convince us about what's real, sometimes it's offering distorted thoughts that affect our emotions and how we choose to act. However, regardless of whether our thoughts reflect reality as it truly is, it's incredibly important for us to tell our stories. This is how we examine life and the world as we know it.

Storytelling isn't a new phenomenon. You may recall, maybe from history classes, that long before people were able to write, they passed stories along orally, through the spoken word. In this way, even the earliest peoples of the earth created a sense of meaning and purpose in their lives.

How Can Storytelling Help You?

You may be thinking, *History is all well and good, but what does this have to do with me?* This chapter provides some guidance on telling the story of your loss as part of your healing journey. Before we get to the details of how to do that, let's take a quick look at the benefits of working on and telling your story.

* **Stories can help you organize bits and pieces of information.** In life, things can happen quickly. And when a brother or sister dies, life can start to feel like one big blur. By exploring the story of your loss, you're giving yourself the time and space to sort through what happened. At the time, events may have seemed to pass so fast that you felt like you were missing them.

* **Stories help you explain your feelings.** So many emotions can crop up as the result of losing a sibling, and it can feel overwhelming when they're caged up inside you. By exploring them in a story, you might be able to sort through your feelings and come to understand why they're so powerful.

* **Stories can help you create a connection with the past.** We tell stories for many reasons, but one is to keep memories alive. By telling the story of your loss, you're connecting with your grief and creating a special place for it as your life moves forward.

* **Stories can bring you closer to other people.** It's hard for others to help you if they don't know what you're going through. By telling your story, you can help the people close to you understand your needs and how they can best support you in the wake of your sibling's death.

* **Stories can help you explore and maybe explain why bad things happen.** The search for meaning is important to most people. As you tell your story and gain some perspective, exploring the details of what happened

might bring you closer to understanding the meaning of your sibling's death.

✳ **Stories can create an ongoing bond with those who have died.** You honor your brother or sister by telling the story of your loss. As long as your story is recounted, your sibling is memorialized.

Perhaps nobody in your life has asked you to tell the story of losing your sibling and how that loss has influenced where you are now. This chapter provides that opportunity. As you do the exercises that follow, always remember that you're the expert. When it comes to telling your story, you're the only one who can do it justice.

Exercise: Preparing to Tell Your Story

Before you start creating your story, take some time to think about how you want to capture and present it. This exercise will help pave the way by asking some questions to get you oriented to the process and helping you gather whatever you need. You might want to keep your journal at hand to jot down any ideas that come up as you consider the questions below. You can also use the worksheet available at http://www.newhar binger.com/32493, "Creating an Outline and Filling In the Details," to help you organize your thoughts.

Are you a writer, a talker, an artist, or somewhere in between?

- **As a writer:** Gather some colorful pens and a notebook.

- **As a talker:** Find an app to record your voice or a digital voice recorder.

- **As an artist:** Surround yourself with your favorite tools to create art. Do you like collage? If so, grab some magazines and newspapers. Maybe oil paints, pastels, or colored pencils make you feel most free to express yourself. Whatever it is that encourages you to create, find it and get ready to use it.

- **As someone who is somewhere in between:** Gather all the materials mentioned above, and also consider other ways to tell your story. For example, you could use music or photography or explore online options, such as creating a blog (which you can share when you're ready).

Do you want to think outside the box? There are many different ways you can tell your story. Beyond the broad categories outlined above, you can take any sort of creative approach that appeals to you:

- Write a letter to yourself from the future or about yourself to someone important in your life. Then take on the role of the recipient and write back. You can continue writing back and forth as many times as you like.

- Write a rap, a rhyming or free-verse poem, or a haiku.

- Interview yourself.

- Create a special certificate highlighting your life achievements, including working toward finding meaning after the loss of your sibling.

- Draw a map of the important places and people in your life, noting any special spots that you and your sibling shared, whether certain rooms or places in your house or parks or recreational areas. Include a key that explains their significance.

- Make a quiz other people can take to see how much they know about your life, complete with a detailed answer key. Include fun facts about your sibling that only you know and that would be interesting for others to learn. This is a unique way of keeping your sibling's memory alive.

- Build a model or use action figures, clay, or other art supplies to represent your story in a 3-D way.

Where do you want to begin and how do you want to structure your story?

- Would you like your story of loss to have a traditional beginning, middle, and end?

- Would you like to start from earlier in your childhood, from the point when your sibling died, or from when the death began to impact you?

- Who are the characters in the story?

- Will you tell your story in the first person, using an "I" voice, or in the third person, as if you were an observer looking in on your life?

- Would you like to tell your story from the point of view of a nontraditional character? For example, the main character in your story can be your grief, or you could tell your story from the point of view of a pet. As long as you document your journey, it doesn't matter whose voice you use to tell your story.

Who's your audience?

- It's helpful to tell your story for yourself, from your own point of view, but perhaps in the future you'd like to share it. If that's the case, who would you like to share your story with?

- Are there lessons you've learned in your journey that might help other teens struggling with the loss of a sibling? Do you have advice to offer?

How Becca, Eric, and Tommy Told Their Stories

In case you need a little help to get going on telling your own story, here are examples of how Becca, Eric, and Tommy told their stories.

✱ *Becca*

I'm a pretty artistic person. I like things that are colorful and draw you in. I decided to use three poster boards to tell my story of what life was like at three times: before Joseph died, right around the time of his death, and after he died. On the first board, I used super bright colors and pictures from magazines of things I love, like fashion and runway shows. I also glued old pictures of my friends on the board. Basically, I created a picture of the life of a girl who was happy and enjoying herself, with lots of friends.

On the second board, I wanted to focus on what it was like for me to learn about Joseph's suicide. I found pictures of art that were really dark—sort of stormy-feeling—and online, I found some poems about what it feels like to be confused and lost. I put lines from the poems into a new document, which I printed, and then I cut out individual words and phrases and glued them all over the board in different places. I thought about drawing Joseph, but it just hurt too much to picture him how he died, so I wrote his name in black with big teardrops coming from the letters.

On the third board, I showed what life was like after Joseph died. I didn't use all the space on the board. I drew myself like a tiny stick figure and drew a gray shadow to represent Joseph's grave. I cut out pictures of people who look sort of like my friends and glued them on the board to make it look like their backs are turned. Then I wrote some words like "Normal?" and "I'm sorry" because those are some of the things I'm thinking about.

Making the story richer: Becca's off to a great start in telling her story with collages and art. It might be useful for her to return to chapter 10 to explore some of her thoughts and feelings about Joseph's death, which she could portray on a fourth poster board. For example, Becca feels very responsible for Joseph's death and thinks she should have stopped it. Might there be a way for her to use a fourth board to tell the story of the people around her, their role in Joseph's death, and how she understands herself now in relation to those people? She might also want to focus on some of her strengths and how she's using them to cope with Joseph's death.

✳ Eric

I guess the biggest question I have since Luke died is who I am now that I don't have my brother. It's tough when I think about telling my story and how I want to do it, because at the end of his life Luke really loved to paint. I like to paint too, but it would be cool to find a way to tell my story that belongs just to me. So I think I'd like to try writing my story in a journal, like a book, for people to read so they can learn about me and what I've been through. I was thinking about how to do this, and I know I tend to focus on Luke a lot, so I thought it would be cool to do something unusual and write a story about all the ways life could look different for me—kind of like those books where you choose a chapter and flip to it and the ending changes.

So what I did was write a bunch of different short stories. In the first one, I'm a kid who never had an amazing older brother and was able to just live his life and be himself. In the second one I'm a kid whose brother died but who had a lot more confidence and didn't totally turn into his brother after the death. That one was actually fun to write because I got to imagine how people in my life would treat me if I didn't focus on Luke so much, and how it would be if I didn't feel so pressured to be like him. I also wrote one from the point of view of Luke watching me from heaven, saying what he might think of how I'm trying to be so much like him. It was cool to think of him that way, laughing at me or saying I'm being lame because I'm trying so hard to be a different person.

Making the story richer: It's a great idea for Eric to write lots of small stories and even try to imagine himself as other characters. But because of how he tries so hard in real life to be like

Luke, it might be especially helpful for him to write about who he actually is, as his own person, exploring what makes him a unique and valuable person. He could write a story introducing readers to who he is and the person he hopes to be. Since it's Eric's story, he's free to choose how to present himself to his readers, and as the writer of the story it's up to him to decide where he wants to focus the story. This is space for Eric, not his brother, and it would be helpful for him to really take ownership of it and write anything about himself he'd like to say.

✽ *Tommy*

I'm stuck on what it was like to see Isla after she died. I think my story needs to be about that so people know what I'm going through and why it's so hard to deal. I'm really into hip-hop these days, so I'm going to try to write my story like a hip-hop song with rhymes and a beat. There are a lot of really good songs where artists talk about what they've been through in life, even really hard things, and I want to do that. I've found a song I like, and I'm going to write my own words to it, all about what happened when Isla died and how it felt and still feels.

Making the story richer: Tommy has vivid memories of what Isla's death was like, but what about the rest of her life? Were there times he shared with Isla that were happy and when he felt safe? If he's telling Isla's story to others, it could be useful for his audience, and for him, to include details about what life was like for them as brother and sister before she died, focusing on some of the happier memories. Also, since Tommy is still struggling with his memories, he might try to add details about what it feels like to experience flashbacks of Isla's death. In addition, he might use the strategies in chapter 10 to help him incorporate some of his thoughts and feelings into the song.

Exercise: Creating an Outline and Filling in the Details

If you feel ready to tell your story, find a quiet, safe place where you can talk out loud, move around, or spend some time writing, painting, singing—whatever you've chosen to do. It's best to set aside a good amount of undisturbed time, or several blocks of time, for telling your story. Also, be aware that telling your story may bring up some strong emotions. If it does, feel free to take a break. At that time, you might want to try some techniques from the section "Finding Healthy Ways to Cope," toward the end of chapter 10.

The following prompts will help you get ready to tell your story. Copy them into your journal and fill in the blanks.

- I want to tell the story about the following time in my life:

- It's important that I write this story because…

- Some worries I have about writing this story are…

- Some positive feelings I have about writing this story are…

- Here's an outline of what my story will include:

- Here's a list of people I might ask to read, listen to, or look at my story—when I'm ready:

- Here's the format I want to use for telling my story:

Now it's time to tell your story. Go for it! You might want to get it out all at once or, as suggested above, work on it over time, focusing on different parts at different times. For example, you could work on it once a day or once a week. Just don't let too much time pass between sessions; you want to keep the momentum moving forward on this project.

Exercise: Taking Time for Reflection

Once you've gotten your story out of your head and into a format that feels right to you, take a step back and look at your creation. Read your story as if you were a stranger, learning about yourself for the first time. Try to approach it with fresh eyes and ask yourself the following questions. You might want to keep your journal at hand for jotting down any ideas that come up as you think about these questions:

- Does your story present a fair view of you as a person, or are there any distorted thoughts? How can you rewrite your story to avoid any distortions and be more fair and balanced?

- How would a stranger summarize your story? Would you be happy with that summary?

- What kind of a character are you in this story? Are you a hero, a villain, or someone in between? Are you okay with that?

- Does this story include all of the important players, or did you leave anybody out?

- Is there room for different points of view in your story, to help your audience understand you more?

- Might you create a prequel or sequel to your story, using your imagination or memories from earlier days?

- Does your story have a traditional beginning, middle, and end? If it doesn't, are you okay with that?

- How do you feel now that your story is out there?

After you've reflected on all of these questions, consider whether you'd like to revise your story in any way. If so, go for it, using the same suggestions from above, taking your time and being gentle with yourself.

✳ *Tommy's Hip-Hop Song*

Tommy incorporated some of the suggestions above, on making his story richer. Then he reflected on it and fine-tuned it. Here's the final product:

"Hey, Isla"
(to the tune of "Hey, Mama," by Kanye West)

Chorus

Hey, Isla,
You left me all alone
To go to your heavenly home.
You never knew what hit you, and now I can't forget you.
Hey, Isla,
Remember back in the day
When you would get afraid
When the lights were out
And we would play monsters and scream and shout?

Verse 1

I wanna tell you 'bout my little sister. (She'll never grow
   a day past her seventh birthday.)
She was a cute kid—so innocent and fun and brave (but
   it's hard to remember her not on the pavement).
But I'll try 'cuz the memories are all I got (and she's so
   much more to me than just a ghost).
Isla, you never even saw the car coming (and I want
   justice so bad it's got me screaming).

(Chorus)

Verse 2

You know I never used to be such a problem child (some
   of my teachers would even call me wild).
Like when I make fun of people in the classroom (or joke
   about having to use the bathroom).
It's just I don't got any other ways to say my feelings
   (and I don't want people feeling sorry for me).
What would you do if you lost a sibling? (And nobody
   knew to ask you, "Hey, how you feeling?")
So I just focus on being the fun guy (and doing other
   things that make me feel all right).
Like leaving home at night or yelling or breaking (all the
   things that used to work, they feel really fake now).

(Chorus)

Verse 3

Now I'm looking 'round and asking those questions
   (about who I am and what will my path be).
I want to try to remember you without the horror ('cuz
   you'll always be my cute little sister).
I want to make you so very proud of your brother (and
   know that I will try to be there for Mom now).
Maybe one day I won't feel so sad and angry (that it's all
   so unfair that this had to happen).
Got to let others know there could be a reason (when
   you see all these bad things just coming at ya).
Got to keep thinking of all of the good times (like
   your birthdays and the way that you danced in the
   sunshine).
On a hot day at the start of the summer season
   (somebody tell me that there just has to be a reason).
Why this perfect little kid could be taken from us (will
   the answer come from somewhere high up above us?).

(Chorus)

How Telling His Story Helped Tommy

Here's how Tommy described his experience with telling
his story:

   *Writing this was really hard for me. I knew I wanted to
write something to the tune of "Hey Mama," because it's a song
by one of my favorite artists who also went through a lot of*

darkness. Aside from that, I didn't know where to start. Then I figured I might as well start with where my mind always goes—to Isla's accident—and then kind of work backward and forward. I tried to keep the happy memories in the chorus because you repeat the chorus, and maybe if I keep trying to focus on the happier times, it will make the harder memories a little weaker. I felt like writing this song was a good way to tell my story to other people. It also made me feel like I got some control back, because nobody else can tell my story but me. In a few weeks or months I want to try to write another verse or two and see if I feel different or if I'd change anything I already wrote. Anyway, overall I think it was a good experience.

Concluding Thoughts

How do you feel about your story, how you chose to tell it, and the details you included? It's important to take some time, as Tommy did, reflecting on both the content of the story and the process of creating it. It's an enormous accomplishment to examine your story of life and loss and then express it in a way that does it justice, and I think you'll find it empowering. Remember, you can always revise your story to account for new lessons you learn about yourself over time or reflections on how you've healed and found new meaning. For that matter, you can even create new stories to reflect your changing experience. It may seem impossible now, but healing will happen, and as it does, your story will change. Your story may be different depending on how you're feeling on a given day. That's fine. What's most important is that you tell it.

chapter 12

Making Meaning

The death of a brother or sister can shake you to your very core. Your understanding of how the world works may have completely changed in the wake of your loss. Many surviving siblings find themselves asking, *Why? Why me? Why our family? Why did this have to happen at all?* These questions can play an important role in your healing. They open the door to a search for meaning. And while these questions can't always be answered, finding reasons why tragedy strikes can be comforting and help you cope. It's human nature to search for meaning in our lives as a pathway to greater understanding. And a lot of times, it comes down to seeing patterns.

Why Patterns Matter

As human beings, we enjoy finding patterns in the world because we like life to be predictable. Think about some of the things you do every day—things you may not think of as giving your life some of the structure we all need: brushing your teeth, taking a shower, going to school, doing chores, or participating in certain activities on a regular basis. Imagine if you suddenly stopped brushing your teeth. All of a sudden, it would feel as though something was missing, wouldn't it? From very simple procedures like taking care of your appearance to deeper areas of your life like love and relationships, it's important to have some predictable and recognizable patterns in your daily life.

The death of a sibling can blow old patterns out of the water and bring about new patterns that may initially feel uncomfortable or even painful. When this happens, life can feel disorganized and confusing. It's good to start recognizing this and noticing how it affects you. The loss of patterns or rituals that once brought certainty and comfort can definitely trigger some big questions about life, loss, and meaning.

Exercise: Noticing Old and New Patterns

This exercise will help you explore how patterns in your life have changed due to the death of your brother or sister. You can use your journal to do it, as described below, or download the worksheet available at http://www.newharbinger.com/32493.

In your journal, write the heading "Old Patterns." Then, underneath that heading, describe some of the rituals and routines that existed before your sibling died. Take your time with this.

When you're finished, write another heading: "New Patterns." Underneath, describe how old patterns have changed since the death of your sibling and list any new patterns that have developed.

Finally, write a third heading: "My Response." For this topic, write whatever thoughts or feelings you have about these changes in patterns.

To help you see how this works, let's take a look at an example from Eric.

Old Patterns

I woke up before Luke every morning at 6:30 and had to wake him up when he slept through his alarm. We walked to school together and would hang out with our friends outside until the first bell rang. We met up with our buddies in the hall between classes and at lunch. After school we played basketball at the community center until about 5:00. After we walked home, I would set the table and Luke would put away the dishes from the dishwasher. We had dinner with Mom and Dad, and sometimes Grandpa would come over. After dinner we'd play video games and then, depending on the night, we'd either do homework or go play some more basketball.

New Patterns

I still wake up at 6:30 a.m., and it's hard to stop myself from going into Luke's room, even though he hasn't been there for a while. When he was sick, there were alarms going off all the time: some for meds, some for appointments, whatever. I don't really hang out with our friends that much before school, like we used to. Instead I spend time with my girlfriend, who used to go out with Luke. Usually we're both late for class. I still go to class, but I feel like everyone is looking at me differently. Now I go to painting classes at the community center after school instead of playing basketball, because Luke really loved to paint when he got too sick to do sports. It doesn't really matter what time I get home, because we don't have dinner together as a family very much anymore, but sometimes my grandpa comes over and hangs out with me. There are lots of dishes piled up in the sink, but unless I do Luke's old job, they just sit there since they can't go in the dishwasher. After dinner I play video games under Luke's old user name, and then I go to bed.

My Response

It's funny. Even though we had new patterns that came up when Luke was sick, he was still a part of it, so I didn't feel so lost. Now it feels like everyone in the house is just kind of doing their own thing, and I'm trying hard to fill the gap where Luke was. I definitely notice that I want things to be the way they were, even though that's impossible. I was really used to having my brother around.

If you haven't already done this exercise yourself, go ahead and do it now, describing old patterns, new ones, and your responses to the changes.

Facing Big Questions

When you were reading Eric's example in the previous exercise, you probably noticed that he's missing not just his brother but also the things they used to do together. Now that old patterns have changed or disappeared, Eric feels lonely and life seems somewhat disorganized. He very well might be asking himself, *Why did my life have to change so much?* Losing Luke and being thrown into a new way of life has probably raised some big questions for Eric.

Exercise: Pondering Your Big Questions

Like Eric, you might be thinking about some big questions these days. (And if you're not thinking about those questions, that's okay too. For now, just consider any exercises or discussions of this topic to be food for thought.) I've listed some of the most common big questions below. Get out your journal or the worksheet available online, and then read through this list and write about any that resonate with you. Feel free to take a lot of time with this exercise. You might want to come back to it repeatedly in the weeks and months to come.

- Why did my sibling have to die?

- Why didn't I die instead?

- What's the point of life if everybody dies?

- What's the meaning of life?

- How can I keep going?

- Will I ever feel better? And is there anything I can do to help me feel better?

- Will I forget my sibling? How can I carry my sibling forward in my heart and mind?

- Is it okay to not think about my sibling all the time? What would my sibling want for me in the weeks and months to come?

These questions are very big and very painful. They all involve a search for meaning and desire for a deeper understanding of your sibling's death. As difficult as it may be to contemplate them, let yourself think about them rather than ignore them.

Sometimes thinking about questions like these can make people feel anxious or overwhelmed. If that happens, return to the breathing exercise in chapter 9 and spend some time focusing on inhaling and exhaling. You might also distract yourself with some of the activities suggested in chapter 10. But once you're feeling more calm, return to this exercise and continue exploring these big questions. It's normal, natural, and healthy to search for meaning in the face of tragedy.

Being You in the Face of Loss

One of the challenges of being a surviving sibling is staying true to yourself while everyone around you is grieving too. And it may be that other people have expectations about how you should act or who you should be now that your brother or sister is gone. It's hard to not feel pressured by those expectations, but remember that being a teen means you're on a search to figure out who you are. It's important to keep focusing on yourself and your feelings, and to keep exploring how you want to move forward in life, even with your grief.

Exercise: Keeping the Focus on You and Your Grief

This exercise will help you tease apart others' expectations of you and your own needs during this difficult time. In your journal, write two headings: "Others' Expectations" and "My Grief." (You can also use the worksheet available online, if that's easier.)

First take some time to think about how others' expectations have affected your grief process. Write down everything you can think of under the heading "Others' Expectations."

Next, turn your focus inward and explore your own grief process, considering your thoughts, feelings, actions, and reactions. Write down everything you can think of under the heading "My Grief." Then write "…and that's okay." If you want, you can even write that after each thing you list.

To see how this works, here's an example from Becca:

Others' Expectations

Want me to take care of my family.

Maybe blame me for my brother's suicide.

Expect me to get good grades.

Ask me questions they should be asking my parents, like how my mom is coping.

My Grief

I feel guilty…and that's okay.

I feel sad…and that's okay.

I feel resentful…and that's okay.

I feel frustrated…and that's okay.

I feel pissed off…and that's okay.

I don't know why this had to happen…and that's okay.

I think it sucks…and that's okay.

Finding Meaning and Purpose

While it's healthy to explore big questions, you can also get stuck in the feelings they bring up. Grief can be open-ended, so it's often hard to feel like there are solid, straightforward answers to the intense feelings that arise. For this reason, it might be helpful to look at your thoughts, feelings, and reactions with the goal of finding the meaning in them. You might be asking yourself, *Is there a greater purpose for me in all the hardship I'm going through right now? What might that be?*

Just to be clear, finding meaning and purpose in your grief doesn't mean you're saying it's okay that your brother or sister died. Rather, you're trying to look at the situation with a new frame of mind, trying to work with it instead of fighting it. Consider this quote by the psychologist and concentration camp survivor Viktor Frankl: "Man's search for meaning…is unique and specific in that it must and can be fulfilled by him alone." This means that only you can find the meaning in your life, and only you can apply that meaning toward a greater purpose.

Exercise: Moving Toward Purpose

In this exercise, you'll begin to look at how you can apply the answers to your big questions to a greater purpose. Take some time to reflect on the following question and write your responses, in your journal or on the worksheet available at the website for this book.

What might the purpose be in all of this, and how could it be useful to me?

As you write, remember that there's no judgment here. You're in your own safe place, writing in your own private journal. Also remind yourself that finding ways to feel better doesn't mean you're ignoring your sibling's death. In fact, your brother or sister would surely want you to find ways to feel better—and want you to find meaning or purpose in his or her death. So stay in the here and now and find your own truth. Here are examples from Becca, Eric, and Tommy.

Becca

What might the purpose be in all of this, and how could it be useful to me?

I've learned how to take care of other people's needs and not always just focus on myself. I'm getting better grades than ever before, and if I do go to college, that means that I can do something with my life that would make my brother proud, like maybe be a counselor to kids who are depressed.

Eric

What might the purpose be in all of this, and how could it be useful to me?

I guess I need to focus more on me and less on Luke and what people think about Luke. Maybe for me this process is all about learning how to survive Luke's death and find that purpose in my own life. I've been leaning on Luke's legacy so much. Maybe it's time for me to focus on my own legacy. If I were to die tomorrow, what would I want people to remember about me? I need to start thinking about that.

Tommy

What might the purpose be in all of this, and how could it be useful to me?

I have so much anger all the time and so many painful memories of what happened to Isla. It's really hard to think that I could find some deeper meaning in all of this. But I can see that my anger is keeping me stuck, so maybe the purpose is learning how to find what makes me happy again.

Pushing Away Big Questions

The kinds of big questions discussed in this chapter can be difficult and painful to grapple with. Sometimes you may just want to hide your head in the sand and block out your awareness of what's happened. That's entirely understandable, but it truly won't help you in the long run. So let's take a look at a few of the ways this kind of avoidance can show up, and then explore whether any of them are a factor for you.

Denial. It might be easier in the short term to pretend that life hasn't changed since your sibling died. Denial can protect you from feelings that are too intense or overwhelming. However, facing these feelings and contemplating the big questions is necessary for long-term healing.

Wishful thinking. Just as with denial, it isn't always a bad thing to wish your life were different or to get caught up in daydreams about how life could be better. But wishful thinking can become a problem if you begin to focus too much on how you think life should be and lose track of the reality that's right in front of you. Starting to contemplate some of your big questions about your sibling's death can help you recognize your current reality and integrate it into your life in a way that works for you. At a more practical level, simply wishing something was different won't make it so. Action is needed.

Compulsive behavior. Compulsive behaviors happen when rituals and routines become too rigid. Instead of just providing comfort, they become limiting. For example, a person with low self-esteem might turn to binge eating when she feels bad because focusing on food provides a distraction from the pain of feeling down on herself. However, it's a stopgap measure that doesn't get to the root of why she has low self-esteem. These types of short-term responses to long-term problems never make the real issues go away. Compulsive behaviors can also arise as a way to avoid grappling with the big questions that come with a loss. Consider Tommy's drinking and risky behaviors. He uses these unhealthy coping strategies to numb out and avoid facing his feelings and fears related to Isla's death. However, these behaviors may eventually result in Tommy seriously hurting himself or others. Until he can look at himself, his memories, and his true feelings, he'll never be able to integrate them into himself in a healthy way. This will be a hard process, and he might need therapy to help him through it.

Exercise: Reflecting on Avoidance

In your journal or on a piece of paper, write three headings: "Denial," "Wishful Thinking," and "Compulsive Behavior." If you want, you could use a separate page for each. Then ask yourself the following questions and record your answers in the appropriate sections. (You can also use the worksheet you'll find at http://www.newharbinger.com/32493.)

Denial. Are you in denial about certain parts of your sibling's death or how it affects your life? How so, and why? What might life look like if you started facing the truth and considering the big questions? How might this be helpful for you?

Wishful thinking. Are you stuck in a pattern of wishful thinking? What are your wishes and daydreams about? Are they helpful to you, or do they keep you from coping with reality? What would it be like if you stopped wishing and started facing life and the big questions that confront you? How would it be helpful for you?

Compulsive behaviors. Have you engaged in any compulsive behaviors in an effort to push away the pain of your loss or other unpleasant emotions that have come up since your sibling's death? Are these behaviors helpful or harmful? Are they perhaps simply distracting you from your feelings and from exploring the big questions? Are there healthier ways to begin to deal with your feelings? What might life look like for you in the long run if you face your feelings?

Deep Thoughts and Deeper Meanings

It's important to begin to recognize how you may have avoided asking big questions in your life. As you begin to move toward finding purpose and embracing these tough topics, you might feel separated from your peers by the big questions going through your head. Some teens find that a sibling's death prompts them to look at life in new ways, and sometimes this can be overwhelming. However, this can also spur you to live life to the fullest as a way of honoring your brother or sister.

In the sections that follow, I'll cover some of the more common deep thoughts and deeper meanings that arise when anyone loses a loved one: fear of death, thoughts about responsibility and personal freedom, thoughts about being isolated, and, sometimes, loss of meaning.

Fear of Death

It isn't surprising that many people, adults included, avoid the topic of death—one of the great unknowns in life. While there are many religious views, spiritual theories, and other ideas about what happens after we die, as of yet there's no definitive answer to the question. Some people seem happy going through life focusing on the here and now, and not the hereafter, whereas others are much more sensitive to the idea of death and have many questions about it. Here are a few that are common:

* Does dying hurt?

* Is there a soul?

* Is death really the end?

* Does heaven exist?

* Is there such a thing as past lives?

Many religious and spiritual concepts of death can be comforting for people who are looking for answers to these questions. However, even for those raised to believe in God or an afterlife, the death of a brother or sister might cause them to question these concepts. Teens naturally question the world around them, including theories about death. You may have watched as your sibling died of an illness, or your sibling's death might have been more sudden. Either way, it's possible that you may have a new fear of death now that you're more closely acquainted with it. Or perhaps you were already fearful of death.

If you're afraid of death, please don't be embarrassed by this. It's far more common than you might think. Here are some ways to cope with a fear of death:

Talk to a religious leader in your community. Seek out different viewpoints from people who follow different religions. Also explore nonreligious views of what happens when we die. Be open to different explanations.

Write about your idea of the afterlife. Do you believe in heaven, angels, or souls? If you believe in an afterlife, imagine your sibling inhabiting it. You might want to write about that, very specifically.

Be okay with not having control. Life and death are governed by immense, complex forces, far beyond any individual's control. So the more you try to exert control in this area, the more frustrated you may become as you discover you simply can't. It might be helpful for you to recite the Serenity Prayer, a classic approach to letting go of things beyond our control: "God, grant me the serenity to accept the things I cannot change, courage to change the things I can, and wisdom to know the difference." If you aren't a religious person, you can leave out the first word and focus on making the prayer more of an affirmation or meditation.

Make a bucket list. Although it might seem morbid to imagine your own death, you might want to make a list of things you'd like to do or see before you die. This can actually help you live life to the fullest and focus on being in the present. Making a bucket list doesn't mean you're going to die soon; it just means you're exploring ways to enjoy being on this earth and making the most of the time you have while you're here. You might even like to put a few things on your bucket list that your brother or sister would have enjoyed, or that you wish you could have done together.

Make a will. You're probably familiar with wills—documents with instructions on how to gift your possessions to your family and friends after you die. Based on what you've experienced with your sibling, you might want to draft your own will. (Not that anything is going to happen to you anytime soon!) This is simply a way of acknowledging what's important to you and whom you'd like to carry those possessions forward when you can't.

Make a living will. A living will documents your wishes if you're ever in a situation where you can't speak for yourself.

This may be especially important to you if you saw your sibling in a medical environment prior to his or her death. Although a living will typically covers things like being on a breathing machine or feeding tube, you could also use it as an opportunity to provide instructions to your family such as "If I'm ever in the hospital, please make sure to bring the following items for me..." Or "I'd like the following people to visit me if I'm ever sick..."

Don't hesitate to ask for help. Sometimes the fear of death can become so overpowering that it's all you can think about. That can definitely stop you from enjoying life. If that happens, please reach out! Talk to a trusted family member, family friend, counselor, or clergyperson. It may be best for a loved one to work with you to find a professional who can help you. There are many therapists who specialize in helping people overcome their fears, including fears brought on by a sibling's death. Grief counseling that includes a focus on the fear of death can be very healing.

Exercise: Reflecting on the Fear of Death

Ask yourself whether you've developed a greater fear of death since your sibling died. In your journal or on the worksheet available online, note which of the strategies discussed above might work for you as a starting point for coping. Then start putting those strategies into action. Or if exploring your fears around death seems too frightening right now, simply list the strategies you think might work for you in the future, when you're feeling more ready.

Thoughts About Responsibility and Personal Freedom

The death of a sibling can also lead you to think about where in your life you have control and where you don't. You may start pondering the concept of responsibility or your accountability for your actions. Additionally, you might wonder how free you are in life to live your dreams and make the most of your life, perhaps in contrast to taking care of others in the wake of your sibling's death. An obvious example is Becca, who now feels responsible for caring for her family. She doesn't feel a great deal of freedom to go out in the world and fulfill her own dreams.

Exercise: Balancing Responsibilities and Dreams

Like Becca, you might benefit from taking a close look at your responsibilities and your dreams for yourself and seeing if you can find a better balance between the two. This exercise will help you do just that. You'll find a worksheet for it online at http://www.newharbinger.com/32493.

Start by making a list of all the responsibilities you think you have. These could be schoolwork, chores, caring for others who are grieving, community service, and the list goes on. Be sure to include any activity you feel you must do to fulfill others' expectations.

For each, consider how much freedo you have. Is it necessary for you to fulfill the responsibility? Are you doing it because you feel you should, or because you genuinely want to or feel it's helpful to your growth as a person?

Next, make a list of your dreams. What are the things you'd really like to do if it were entirely up to you?

Now consider which is more important: being free to achieve whatever you want or having some level of responsibility in your life. Like most people, you'll probably decide it's best to seek a balance between the two. If you're only fulfilling tasks and duties that others expect of you, you may want to include more activities that you enjoy and that help make your life more fulfilling, and vice versa.

When Becca did this exercise, she decided to enroll in a weekly modern dance class as a way of shifting the balance more toward her own needs and dreams. Tommy, on the other hand, realized that he needed to be more responsible, including focusing in class and not being so disruptive.

Thoughts About Being Isolated

It's been said that dying is the loneliest human experience, yet it may be lonelier to live on, without a loved one. Isolation is any feeling of loneliness and being separate from other people, whether due to geography, conflicted feelings about relationships with others, or lack of social skills. And sometimes it's easier to stay isolated from others than to become involved in the living, breathing world around you. By being alone and focusing on yourself, you don't have to deal with others' expectations or their questions or feelings about your sibling's death.

However, human beings are social animals. We enjoy being in close contact with others, and we need that contact. True, some people need more personal space, but most of us benefit from finding the time to connect with other people. Being isolated can leave you living in your own head, stuck in a spin cycle with your thoughts and feelings and disconnected from reality. Here are some strategies for moving away from isolation and toward finding some support:

* Seek out online resources. The Dougy Center is a great place to start (http://www.dougy.org/grief-resources/help-for-teens).

* Find a local support group. You may want to do an Internet search for "teen grief group" and your zip code. There may be a group for people just like you at a local hospital, hospice, or community center, where you can connect with others who have had similar experiences.

* Start a blog or website. One way to reach out to others is to share your own experiences, including in an online journal or blog or by creating your own website. You might end up with followers who can identify with the path you're on.

* Post about your experience on Facebook or Twitter. Sometimes it's easier to share a few short sentences about what you're going through, rather than trying to talk about it with individual friends face-to-face. Try posting about your feelings and why you're feeling that way. For example, you might say, "I'm feeling sad today, like nobody understands what it's like to lose a sibling." You might be surprised at how many of your friends and followers respond and provide sympathy and support.

✳ Get out of the house and allow yourself to be distracted. It's okay to not always think about your feelings and your loss. This is different from denial, where you're purposely and consistently ignoring what's going on inside you. What I'm suggesting here is to devote maybe an hour of the day to sports, creative tasks, volunteering, or other activities that put you in contact with other people. By focusing on other aspects of your life and health, you'll create more balance and a better state of mind to deal with what's going on inside.

Exercise: Reflecting on Isolation

To reflect on whether feelings of isolation are a factor for you, ask yourself the following questions and write your responses in your journal or on the worksheet you'll find online:

- Are you spending more and more time alone, away from others?

- Do you feel as though nobody else can understand what you're going through?

- Is it helpful for you to be this isolated, or would you like to connect more with others?

- Which strategies for connecting and seeking support might work for you, and why? Go through the list above and jot down any that you'd like to try in your journal. Also list your own ideas.

Loss of Meaning

Although losing a sibling can create motivation to search for meaning and purpose in life, some people initially find that it erases all sense of meaning from their life. Death is a tough reality to face. It can create feelings of helplessness, hopelessness, anger, anxiety, and depression. These emotions can put you in a very dark place where, instead of asking, *Why did this have to happen?* you might start to say, *There's no reason for this. Life has no meaning.* Thinking these thoughts and experiencing the emotions they stir up can leave you paralyzed with fear or truly despairing. This kind of loss of meaning can sometimes cause people to feel as if there's no hope for the future; they might even consider suicide as a way out.

When people experience a loss of meaning, they often lose their sense of purpose, lose sight of goals, and question the point of everything and anything. If you're going through this very painful experience, please know that you aren't alone. Here are a few things you can do:

* Review the previous sections under "Deep Thoughts and Deeper Meanings" for ideas about how to cope, connect with others, and face your feelings.

* Create a mantra you can use when your thoughts spiral to dark places. Choose something positive, soothing, or motivating, then write it down. When you feel overwhelmed, look it at, recite it, or think about it. Here are some ideas:

"This too shall pass."

"It gets better."

"The night is always darkest before the dawn."

* If you're thinking about ending your life, please call the National Suicide Prevention Lifeline, at 1-800-273-8255 (TALK) or visit their website (http://www.suicide preventionlifeline.org) and chat online. You'll find someone supportive to connect with, 24/7.

* If you're harming yourself in other ways, check out the organization To Write Love on Her Arms (http://www .twloha.com). This is a group for young people that focuses on suicide and self-harm prevention. Their web-site features guest blogs and resources for teens who are struggling. Check out the "Find Help" link for helplines and other sources of support, or just explore the site to find helpful information.

* Write about your feelings and experiences. Keeping a journal is a way of honoring your path and safely explor-ing deep questions as you try to find renewed mean-ing in life. You can also express yourself by drawing, creating a scrapbook, or using other creative methods of expressing yourself (see chapter 11). One of the most powerful ways of finding purpose is to give yourself a voice and speak your truth.

* Consider going to therapy. Realizing that you can't get through this alone is a huge step. It's also a sign of strength and resourcefulness. If you find yourself spending more and more time feeling hopeless and helpless, know that working with a therapist might help

you start to feel better again. Talk to a teacher, parent, or other trusted adult about what you're going through and let that person know you need help. If you don't know what words to use, here are a few ways to start the conversation:

"I'm really struggling with my sibling's death. I think I need to talk to someone, like a therapist or counselor."

"I need help. I need to talk to someone about my feelings."

"It's hard for me to say this, but I need someone to talk to."

"I can't do this alone anymore. I think I might hurt myself."

"Can you help me find a therapist who specializes in talking to teens?"

Concluding Thoughts

My hope is that this chapter helped you explore some of the elements of your grief that run more deeply. Facing your grief and the big questions it brings up can be overwhelming at times. It can be easier to opt for denial, avoidance, or distraction with unhealthy compulsive behaviors. However, over time these strategies will probably stop working, so you'll still face questions about deeper meanings. You may still have to cope with fears of death, a sense of isolation, or actually losing a sense of meaning. It's healthier to go ahead and face the big questions as they arise than to pretend they don't exist, even though doing so can be extremely difficult. Asking for help can be hard too, but it may be a necessary step on your journey. Remember the saying "The journey of a thousand miles begins with a single step." The question is, are you ready to take that first step? I think you are. In fact, by reading and working with this book, you already have.

chapter 13

What Next?

You've arrived at the last chapter of this book. Hopefully you've learned that you aren't alone in this journey. There are other teens who walk this path—even though it's a path nobody should have to walk. There are many caring, supportive adults who want to help. There are also many ways to cope with your grief. Still, recognizing that you need help isn't easy, nor is finding the words to talk about your feelings and experiences. Change can be frightening, and even after everything you've read in this book, you may still think it's easier to suffer in silence. I understand, but please don't go it alone. And don't let your grief remain unexpressed.

Traveling down the path of healing means looking at your thoughts, feelings, actions, assumptions, and the world around you. It means being active in challenging distorted thoughts and examining painful questions about life and death. You may sometimes slip backward as you ride the waves of grief, but as long as you keep expressing your truth, you're healing.

Carrying Your Memories While Being Uniquely You

I want to stress again that traveling this healing path doesn't mean leaving your sibling behind or forgetting about him or her. Wherever you go in life, wherever your journey may take you, you'll carry your sibling with you. At times, your memories might feel overwhelming and sad, but eventually you'll be able to bring more focus to the happier aspects of your sibling's life and your experiences together. As you ask yourself, *Who am I?*, it's okay to answer that question, in part, with "a grieving sibling." But it's also important to think about the other parts of you that make you uniquely *you*.

Exercise: Who Are You?

Really reflect on the question "Who am I?" Then, in your journal, list some of the many qualities and characteristics that make you the only *you* that could ever exist in this world. Really take your time with this. Also remember that your journal is a safe and private place, just for you. So feel free to write anything and everything.

How do you feel after completing this exercise? My hope is that you'll start to create a picture of yourself that includes the impact of your sibling's death but that doesn't neglect the other important pieces of you.

Talking About Your Loss with Others

An important part of your healing journey may be sharing about yourself and your experience of grief with important people in your life. People might ask lots of different questions about your story or respond to it in different ways, but now you're prepared to face those kinds of queries. And ultimately, the main thing is to tell it, giving voice to your experiences and opening the door to discussing your grief so you won't feel so isolated and alone. In this section, I'll share a few tips for talking about your grief.

Use "I" Statements

It's important that you stay true to yourself. Although others in your life may have influenced your feelings, the most genuine way to express your truth is to start with "I." For example, when Becca first approached her mom to talk about her grief, she said, "I feel very alone in this struggle. I feel like I'm caring for you instead of focusing on being a normal teenager." Because Becca is using "I" statements and taking ownership of her emotions (by saying "I feel"), she isn't accusing her mother of purposefully neglecting her, even though she might feel that way. This can help her mother not feel attacked, paving the way for a genuine dialogue in which her mother can listen to her perspective without closing down.

Be Specific About Your Needs

As you open up to talking about your loss, people may ask, "How can I help you?" or "Is there anything you need?" It's best to respond with specific ways a given person can support you as you cope with grief. For example, Tommy told his teachers that he needed extensions on some of his assignments because he was having a hard time focusing, so it was taking longer for him to get his work done. Eric told his grandfather, "I need help with the dishes. Luke used to put them away, and I just can't face doing it now."

Consider what people can do to ease your burden. It's okay to ask for help. In fact, people love showing they care by doing things that might be too overwhelming for you right now. It's also okay to express less specific needs. For example, Becca told her dad, "I just need someone to sit with me, listen to me, and hold my hand when I cry." Knowing that, Becca's dad made the time to just be there for her.

Learn How to Say No

Part of learning about who you are in the wake of your loss is putting up healthy boundaries. You don't have to do everything that's asked of you, especially in situations where you feel vulnerable, uncomfortable, or pressured. Some of us are raised to think that saying no means we're rude, disobedient, inflexible, or maybe incompetent. But there are plenty of times when saying no is appropriate.

For example, Tommy started to realize that drinking and smoking pot were actually keeping him stuck in his grief. As a first step, he started trying to say no at parties when his friends were pushing him to do more. Peer pressure made it hard, especially since he'd created an image of himself of a bad boy who didn't care. So now he's working on avoiding these situations altogether, just walking away before the situation comes up.

Likewise, Eric quit hosting cancer survivor meetings in his family's living room. At first he felt he was letting Luke and the cancer community down, but he bolstered himself with reminders that he needs to spend more time working on exploring who he is. When he feels more confident about his own identity, Eric might return to hosting those events every now and then, or he might find other ways to work in the cancer survivor community. But for now, he thinks Luke would be proud of him for taking a stand for himself.

Try to Understand but Detach from Other Points of View

Not everybody is going to understand your grief journey, and other people will have their own feelings and process. It's always helpful to be open to what others are thinking and feeling and to support them in whatever they're going through. But that doesn't mean you have to believe their perspective represents some sort of absolute truth. In fact, as you now know, this can lead to distorted thoughts if you internalize how you think others expect you to feel or act.

Consider Becca. Her mother told her, "I don't think I'll ever be able to move forward in life without your brother." That was a devastating thing for Becca to hear. Becca could have interpreted that statement as implying that she would have to take care of her mother forever, or that she alone isn't enough to make her mother want to move forward in life. But Becca simply received her mother's statement and responded, "I hear you saying that think you won't be able to move forward. But I want to move forward in my life, and I want to do that without feeling like I'm leaving you behind." In this way, Becca echoed her mother's statement and showed that she heard and understood it, but she also asserted herself—again, by using "I" statements.

Exercise: Coming Up with Some Talking Points

Based on everything you've read in this section on talking about your loss with others, take some time to think about how you might implement the strategies outlined above. Ask yourself the following questions, and jot down your responses in your journal:

- What are some "I" statements you can come up with for starting conversations about your loss with family members, friends, and other people who care about you? How can you state your feelings right now?

- What are some specific kinds of help you could ask for right now? Are there different things you'd like to ask for from different people? As you write your ideas, keep all sorts of people in mind: friends, family members, teachers, clergy, neighbors—anyone who's important in your life.

- What are some areas in your life where it might be helpful to say no? If you currently aren't saying no, what's stopping you? How can you feel more empowered to say no?

- Have others recently said things that were hard for you to take in or detach from? How can you listen openly and understand them while staying true to yourself?

When to Ask for Help

All of the chapters in part 3 offered approaches you can use to work toward healing. Occasionally I provided information on resources, including online resources, that might be available to help you cope with your grief. Sometimes it can be hard to know when you may need to reach out to others to ask for more help. Working with this book is a great beginning, but if you continue to struggle, please continue your journey by seeking other forms of help. How can you know if this would be a good idea? Here are a few warning signs that can alert you to this:

* Continuing to cut yourself off from others and isolate yourself because you feel nobody understands

* Thinking about hurting yourself in any way, whether cutting, burning, or making a plan for suicide

* Having more panic attacks or nightmares

* Crying more or having increasing feelings of sadness, hopelessness, or helplessness—or any other feelings— that make it hard for you to focus or that often interrupt your life

* Having intrusive thoughts about your sibling that you can't get out of your head

* Feeling interested in therapy or talking to others who might get it, or just feeling the need for support

The list above isn't exhaustive. The main point is to ask for help when you need it. Your first priority has to be taking care of *you*.

Exercise: Identifying Who Can Help You

Take some time to list people in your life you might ask for help. They might be family members, friends, or other trusted adults. Write that list in your journal now so it will be handy anytime you need it. You might also write what type of help you'd want to seek from each person.

Spooky and Spiritual Experiences

After a loved one dies, some people report unusual experiences that involve the person who died. There's a lot of variety in these experiences, and they may be either comforting or unsettling—or both at the same time. Here are a few of the most common experiences:

* The loved one visiting in a dream

* The loved one appearing like a ghost at the edge of your bed

* Seeing your loved on out of the corner of your eye or passing by on the street

* Hearing your loved one's voice in your head

* Seeing signs that it seems your loved one has left, perhaps in the form of certain animals, colors, rainbows,
stormy weather, and so on

If you've had any experiences along these lines, don't worry.
Many people have these experiences and find them comforting. However, our culture generally teaches us to not believe in
ghosts, so if you've had these kinds of experiences, you might
be inclined to focus on whether your brain is fooling you or
you're hallucinating, rather than just appreciating the comfort
these experiences can bring.

Rather than worrying, consider exploring these experiences. Might they be telling you something about yourself, your
feelings, or the importance of your brother or sister in your life?
Might they be a way of feeling a connection, even now that your
sibling is gone? Here are some avenues for exploration:

* Keep a journal documenting dates, times, and details of
these experiences. Review them for patterns. For example, do they happen when you're extremely upset, at
night, or randomly?

* Explore your spiritual or religious beliefs. Were you
raised to believe that these types of experiences are an
expression of the deceased person's spirit? Has anyone
in your family experienced similar events?

* How do you feel after these experiences? Are they comforting to you? Do you look forward to them? Or are
they frightening?

There are many books that address this issue, like *Hello from
Heaven!*, a collection of stories about after-death communication

that might normalize the situation for you. You might want to search the Internet for "after-death communication" to see if there are any websites about this that you can relate to.

Most of all, don't jump to the conclusion that there's something wrong with you if you've had an experience along these lines that you can't quite explain. As a rule, if the experience is helpful and comforting, that's not a bad thing; you don't need to seek help unless you'd like to share or discuss the experience with others. That said, you may want to speak to a clergyperson or talk to a trusted friend about what you experienced. And if you're finding these experiences frightening, unsettling, or confusing, or if they're taking up a lot of your time, isolating you from other people, interfering with your daily life, or taking over your thoughts, it's probably a good idea to seek help.

Staying Connected with Your Sibling

Sometimes when people *don't* have the kinds of experiences described above, they feel disconnected from their loved one. They're aware of these kinds of "visitations" and wish for one themselves. If that's the case for you, be assured that you don't need such experiences to stay connected with your brother or sister. There are many ways to keep your sibling in your daily life. Here are a few suggestions based on great research by Nancy Hogan and Lydia DeSantis, professors who specialize in this topic.

Tell your sibling what's going on with you. You can still write letters to your sibling or just talk out loud to your brother or sister at the end of the day. You can write songs or poems with your brother or sister in mind. If you pray, include your sibling in your prayers. It's totally okay to speak to your sibling as if he or she is still here. You never know if you might be heard.

Try to understand. Revisit chapter 12 and keep looking for meaning to help you cope with your loss. Imagine your sibling on his or her own cosmic journey of self-discovery. Ask yourself, *What have I learned from this experience? Why do I think it happened? How can I learn from it?*

Look for influence. Are there ways that your brother or sister can still play a role in your life? Without going overboard with this, are there certain parts of your sibling's personality that you'd like to adopt or activities you'd like to do in your sibling's honor? In certain situations, you may want to ask yourself, *I wonder what my sibling would do?* Keep a picture of your sibling close by or create an image or symbol to remind you of your brother or sister every time you see it. Just keep in mind, as discussed in chapter 6, "The Replacement," that this isn't a healthy strategy if you spend too much time trying to be like your brother or sister and lose yourself in the process.

Move away from guilt. If you're stuck in thoughts of guilt and regret, recognize that this isn't healthy for you and won't foster a healthy relationship with the memory of your brother or sister. Ask yourself, *How would my sibling want me to feel about our relationship?* It's unlikely that your brother or sister would want you to feel guilt or regret. Picture hopeful or helpful things that your sibling might say to you, like "You can make it!" "Try to have some fun" or "I love you!" You might even imagine a reunion with your sibling one day. What might he or she say to you as the two of you look back on your lives together?

Be Proud of Yourself

You've been through one of life's most painful experiences—one that's inevitable, but that no one should ever have to go through: the death of a loved one. Be proud of yourself for your strength, the way you've kept your sibling's memory alive, and everything you've accomplished here in this book. Exploring grief is never easy. I hope this book has provided some support as you've learned to understand your loss, incorporate it into your life, and work toward healing.

I'm grateful that you picked this book up, and I hope it's been helpful. Please keep me posted by e-mail or on Facebook with how you're doing as you continue to grieve, cope, and find meaning after loss.

Erica Goldblatt Hyatt, DSW, is assistant professor and department chair of psychology at Bryn Athyn College. Over the course of her career, she has served as a hospital administrator, mental health clinician, academic advisor, family-informed trauma treatment therapist, and clinical oncology social worker to both adult and pediatric populations.

To contact Goldblatt Hyatt, you can reach her at Doctor.Erica@icloud.com, or find her on Facebook at www.facebook.com/doctorEricaGHyatt.

Foreword writer **Kenneth J. Doka, PhD**, is professor of gerontology at the Graduate School of The College of New Rochelle, and senior consultant to the Hospice Foundation of America. He is author of *Improving Care for Veterans Facing Illness and Death*, *Ethics and End-of-Life Care*, and more.

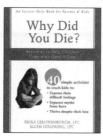
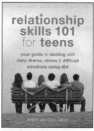

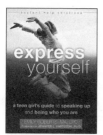

ARE YOU SEEKING A CBT THERAPIST?

The Association for Behavioral & Cognitive Therapies (ABCT) Find-a-Therapist service offers
a list of therapists schooled in CBT techniques. Therapists listed are licensed professionals who
have met the membership requirements of ABCT and who have chosen to appear in the directory.

Please visit www.abct.org and click on *Find a Therapist*.

Register your **new harbinger** titles for additional benefits!

When you register your **new harbinger** title—purchased in any format, from any source—you get access to benefits like the following:

- Downloadable accessories like printable worksheets and extra content
- Instructional videos and audio files
- Information about updates, corrections, and new editions

Not every title has accessories, but we're adding new material all the time.

Access free accessories in 3 easy steps:

1. Sign in at NewHarbinger.com (or **register** to create an account).

2. Click on **register a book**. Search for your title and click the **register** button when it appears.

3. Click on the **book cover or title** to go to its details page. Click on **accessories** to view and access files.

That's all there is to it!

If you need help, visit:

NewHarbinger.com/accessories

new harbinger
CELEBRATING
40 YEARS